PRAY BOLD

DARE TO ASK AND BELIEVE BIG

JOEL OSTEEN

NEW YORK · NASHVILLE

ALSO BY JOEL OSTEEN

PRAY
BOLD

FaithWords
Hachette Book Group
1290 Avenue of the Americas, New York, NY 10104
faithwords.com
@FaithWords / @FaithWordsBooks

First Edition: January 2025

FaithWords is a division of Hachette Book Group, Inc. The FaithWords name and logo are registered trademarks of Hachette Book Group, Inc.

The publisher is not responsible for websites (or their content) that are not owned by the publisher.

The Hachette Speakers Bureau provides a wide range of authors for speaking events. To find out more, go to hachettespeakersbureau.com or email HachetteSpeakers@hbgusa.com.

FaithWords books may be purchased in bulk for business, educational, or promotional use. For information, please contact your local bookseller or the Hachette Book Group Special Markets Department at special.markets@hbgusa.com.

Library of Congress Cataloging-in-Publication Data
Names: Osteen, Joel, author.
Title: Pray bold : dare to ask and believe big / Joel Osteen.
Description: First edition. | New York : Faith Words, 2025.
Identifiers: LCCN 2024032474 | ISBN 9781546005155 (hardcover) | ISBN 9781546005179 (ebook) | ISBN 9781546008279 (large print)
Subjects: LCSH: Prayer. | Faith. | Christian life.
Classification: LCC BL560 .O486 2025 | DDC 248.3/2—dc23/eng/20240830
LC record available at https://lccn.loc.gov/2024032474

ISBNs: 9781546005155 (hardcover); 9781546008279 (large print); 9781546005179 (ebook), 9781546009184 (international trade)

Printed in the United States of America

LSC-C

Printing 1, 2024

CONTENTS

INTRODUCTION

Have you ever wondered why we so seldom see God do great things? Perhaps you heard or read about someone else's remarkable answer to a prayer, and you asked yourself how that person had the faith to pray that boldly. Maybe you're wondering what makes that person's prayers so powerful and effective.

If that's you, you're not alone. In Luke 11, it says that after the disciples watched Jesus praying in a certain place, they were stirred with a desire to pray like He did. They recognized the intimacy of His prayers to His Father, how vital it was to His life, how bold He was in what He asked for, which was so different from the morning and evening prayers the Pharisees and religious leaders recited in the synagogues. It was how Jesus prayed, and what Jesus prayed, that impressed them to ask Him to teach them to pray.

Jesus taught them what we know now as the Lord's Prayer. He started off saying, "Our Father in Heaven." The prayer goes on to talk about our daily bread, protection from evil, and forgiving others. But it's significant that before we ask for our needs, before we ask for protection and guidance, God says, "I want you to acknowledge who you are. I want you to see yourself as My child." Learning to pray bold begins with saying, "God, I know who I am. I belong to You. You're my Father. You created me. You love me. You care for me. You protect me. You favor me." If you don't know who you are, the rest of this prayer is not going to be effective. Because you know you're His child, you can ask in faith for your daily bread, your protection, and your guidance. Because of who you are, you can stay in peace, knowing that your Father will do for you more than you can ask, think, or imagine.

I've learned that how you pray determines what kind of life you live. If you only pray small, ordinary, get-by prayers, you'll live a small, ordinary, get-by life. There is nothing wrong with those prayers, but Scripture says that God is able to do exceedingly abundantly above all we can ask or think. When you have the boldness to ask the Creator of the universe, the Most High God, your Father in Heaven, for big things, you will see the greatness of God's power and love.

In this book, you will discover how to pray God-sized prayers. I will challenge you to ask for the abundant, overflowing, more-than-enough life that God has for you. To do that, you may have to stop letting your circumstances, or what you've believed in the past, or any negative mindsets, to keep you praying weak prayers. God is listening and waiting for you to pray for your dreams, for the big things on your heart.

If you want to make God happy, if you want to put a smile on His face, it's time to take the limits off and dare to pray bold. But before you get started, just let me pray over you:

> *Lord God, thank You for who You are, our Father in*
> *Heaven, and for all You've done in making us Your sons*
> *and daughters. Thank You that we can know You, the Most*
> *High God, and come into Your presence with boldness and*
> *gladness. We know You're here with us right now, and we*
> *worship You. We love You because You first loved us and*
> *chose us. We recognize every good thing has come from*
> *You, and we thank You for the new things You're doing*
> *right now. We invite You to take the reading of the words*
> *of this book and do exceedingly more than any of us could*
> *ever hope or imagine. Breathe upon us and open our eyes to*

a fresh vision of the abundant life that You have called us to. Help us to let go of all the old negative thoughts about prayer and never settle for a small view of You. Help us to start thinking as You think, to think big, to think increase, to think breakthrough, to think victory. Thank You for Your unlimited supply of everything we need in this life. Increase our capacity to believe and receive. We're taking the limits off because we know all things are possible to You. In Jesus' name, Amen.

PRAY
BOLD

CHAPTER ONE

Dare to Pray Boldly

When you know who our God is, you'll take the limits off and ask Him for your dreams, for what looks impossible, for the big things He has put in your heart.

One reason we don't see God do great things is we're only asking for small things. We pray over our food, we pray for protection, we pray for wisdom, and that's all good. But when was the last time you asked God to do something that seems impossible, out of the ordinary, something you couldn't accomplish on your own? If God answered everything you're praying about now, would it be big enough, would you be satisfied? Are you asking for your dreams? Are you asking for something that's over your head? Are you asking for the secret petitions you know that He's put in your heart but you haven't told anyone else about? They seem too far out, unthinkable.

Many prayers are not being answered simply because they're not being asked. If you only pray small prayers, you're not going to see the greatness of our God. If you only ask for little things, you're not going to reach the fullness of your destiny. There are dreams God has put in your heart and obstacles that you'll face that are too big for you to overcome by yourself. If you

> Many prayers are not being answered simply because they're not being asked.

don't learn to pray bold prayers, if you don't learn to ask big, to ask for your dreams, you'll get stuck where you are.

"Joel, God has more important things to deal with than this." You are not inconveniencing God by praying boldly. Bold prayers get God's attention. Bold prayers cause angels to go to work. Bold prayers open doors you could never open. Bold prayers turn impossible situations around. When you pray boldly, you're releasing your faith. You're saying, "God, I know there's nothing too hard for You. I know that You're the all-powerful, Creator of the universe. You can take me where I can't go on my own."

What Do You Want?

God says in Psalm 2, "You're My child. What do you want? Ask Me, and I'll give you nations as a present. I'll give you continents as a prize." We're asking for small things, such as, "God, help me to make ends meet. Help me to live with this sickness. Help me to endure this job." God is saying, "I have nations for you. I have something awesome in your future, something bigger than you've imagined, but there's a condition. You have to ask." You're not going to see the nations, you won't see the continents as a prize, if you're praying small, weak, limited prayers. "God, You know about the gas prices, inflation, and the recession. Help me to make my house payment this month." That's an ordinary prayer. A bold prayer is: "God, help me to pay off my house. Help me to have overflow so I can pay off someone else's house." A normal prayer is: "God, my child is off course. Help him not to get in trouble. Keep him out of harm's way."

> You're not going to see the nations, you won't see the continents as a prize, if you're praying small, weak, limited prayers.

That's good, but ordinary prayers get ordinary results. If you only pray small, you'll only receive small. A bold prayer is: "God, I'm asking You to not just protect my child but help him to fulfill his destiny. Use him in great ways to make a difference with his life." Maybe you've been through disappointments, and life has thrown you curves. A normal prayer is: "God, just help me to survive. Help me to endure." A bold prayer is: "Father, You say You will give me double for the unfair things that have happened. You say You have beauty for these ashes. So, Lord, thank You that something awesome is coming my way."

James 4 says, "You ask and do not receive, because you ask amiss." The word *amiss* means "sick, weak, miserable." This is saying that you won't receive when you pray sick prayers, when you pray weak prayers. When we pray to survive, to endure, to just make it through, that's a sick prayer. "God, I'm so defeated. I'm under so much pressure. You have to do something." That prayer needs to go to Urgent Care. That prayer is on its last leg. Try a different approach, a bold prayer. "God, I have a lot coming against me, but I know Your being for me is greater than what's trying to stop me. Lord, thank You that the tide of the battle is beginning to turn right now." That's a healthy prayer. That gets God's attention. He responds to faith-filled prayers.

> That prayer needs to go to Urgent Care. That prayer is on its last leg.

Sometimes what we call prayer is really a complaint session. "God, the people at work are getting on my nerves. My children don't appreciate me. My back's hurting. My husband's been rude. The dog doesn't like me, and the goldfish is depressed. God, You have to do something." That's a sick prayer. You need to pray from a place of faith. You don't have to tell God all your problems. He already knows everything that's going on. Ask Him for what you want Him to do. Ask Him for what you're believing for. "God, I'm up against all this trouble, but thank You that You are turning it around and fighting my battles. I know that You'll bring me out better than I was before."

In John 4, Jesus had traveled to a city in Samaria. His disciples went into town to get food while He sat at a well waiting for them. A woman came to get water, and Jesus asked her for a drink. She said, "Sir, you're a Jew, and I'm a Samaritan woman. Why are You asking me for a drink?" Back then, Jewish men refused to have anything to do with Samaritan men, let alone women. Jesus said to her, "If you only knew who I am and how generous our God is, you would ask Me and I would give you living water." She said, "But You don't even have a bucket. How would You get this living water?" She was thinking about water in the well, something ordinary. But Jesus said, "If you knew who I was, you wouldn't ask Me for water. I have so much more. I can give you living water." When you know who our God is, when you realize that He created the universe, spoke worlds into existence, parted the Red Sea, healed lepers, multiplied food, and closed the mouths of lions, you won't just ask Him for water, for ordinary things. You'll ask Him for living water. You'll ask Him for your dreams. You'll ask Him for what looks impossible. Are you like this lady, asking Him for water, asking Him for the ordinary? He's saying, "I have living water. I have abundance. I have healing. I have breakthroughs. I have houses. I have businesses. I have ministries. I have favor that will catapult you where you can't go by yourself."

> **When you know who our God is, when you realize that He created the universe, spoke worlds into existence, parted the Red Sea, healed lepers, multiplied food, and closed the mouths of lions, you won't just ask Him for water, for ordinary things.**

Be Strong and Do Exploits

The Scripture says, "The people who know their God will be strong and do exploits." When you know who you're talking to, you won't pray weak prayers or sick prayers. You'll pray bold prayers. You'll ask for things that other people think are far out, too much, that could never happen. Bold prayers get bold results. I wouldn't be doing what I'm doing today if I hadn't learned this principle to ask God for big things, for things that seemed over my head, but I knew deep down God put them in my heart. I don't want to come to the end of life and wonder what would have happened if I had prayed boldly, believed big, and taken the limits off God.

Three years after my father passed and I had stepped up to pastor the church, a friend called and said the Houston Rockets basketball team was moving out of their building, the former Compaq Center, and it was going to be put up for sale. When I heard that, something came alive inside. I knew it was supposed to be ours. But everything in my mind said, "There's no way the city council is ever going to let a church have this building. Besides, you're not qualified, and you don't have the money. How would you be able to pay for it?" But God will put things in your heart on purpose that are too big for you, over your head, that seem impossible. That's a test. Are you going to talk yourself out of it? Are you just going to ask for water? Are you going to just ask for the normal? Or are you going to recognize the One who's putting that dream in you? Are you going to recognize who you're dealing with, the all-powerful Creator of the universe? When you do, you'll ask Him for living water. I said, "God, this is over my head, but I know it's not over Your head. We

> God will put things in your heart on purpose that are too big for you, over your head, that seem impossible.

don't have the funds, but I know that You own it all. God, those who are opposing us are bigger and stronger, but I know Your being for us is more powerful than what's coming against us."

On nights when there were no events in the Compaq Center, Victoria and I would walk around the building and thank God that He was making a way where we didn't see a way. Against all odds, doors opened, the right people showed up, and God gave us the building. Are you praying any bold prayers? Are you believing for anything that's out of reach? Your mind says, "There's no way." Maybe it's to set a new standard for your family. "God, let me rise out of this lack and mediocrity. Let me leave an inheritance to my children's children." Or, "God, let me own my own business. Let me build that orphanage. Let me be free from this illness." You won't see the great things if you're only praying for small things.

> **Are you believing for anything that's out of reach?**

Ask for Your Dreams

Many times when the people in the Old Testament were up against a big challenge, they would start their prayer by talking about the greatness of God. In 2 Chronicles 20, King Jehoshaphat and the people of Judah had three armies surrounding them and quickly closing in. He gathered the people at the city square in Jerusalem, and they looked up to the heavens. Jehoshaphat didn't say, "God, where are You? Do You see what's happening? We're about to be captured." Rather, he said, "O Lord, You alone are God. You are the ruler over all the kingdoms of the nations. You are so powerful and mighty that no one can stand against You. We remember how You brought us through war, through famine, through disease. Now we're asking

You, our great God, to deliver us from these mighty armies." When you remind yourself of who you're dealing with, you won't pray weak prayers. You won't pray sick prayers. You'll pray boldly. You'll ask God to do the impossible, what seems unlikely. Those are prayers that get God's attention. The people of Judah didn't even have to fight. The three enemy armies turned on one another and ended up destroying themselves.

I met a young lady after one of our church services who didn't speak English when she came here with her family from South America. She started coming to Lakewood and listened through headphones to the services translated in Spanish. One Sunday, she heard me talking about praying bold prayers and believing for the dreams God put in your heart. She had always wanted to start a business to help people learn how to speak English. She said, "In that service, for the first time, I said, 'God, I want to own my own business. Help me to make it happen.'" At that time she was trying to learn English but couldn't yet speak it. But she knew that this was something God dropped in her spirit. What activated her faith was when she had the boldness to ask for it. She dared to ask for what seemed impossible. Fourteen years later, this lady has an incredibly successful business. She has taught thousands of people to speak English and says, "God has done so much more than I ever imagined."

I wonder if there are dreams locked up in you that you've never asked for. Are there Compaq Centers for which you've never dared to say, "God, let it happen"? Is there a healing, a business, a spouse, or freedom from an addiction that God is just waiting for you to be bold enough to ask Him for? It may seem over your head, too far out, and every circumstance says it will never happen, but do you realize who you're dealing with? Don't go your whole life asking God for water when He has living water, something you've never experienced—supernatural favor, supernatural increase, supernatural healing. When your mind tries to talk you out of it, you have to do as

Jehoshaphat did and say, "O Lord God, there is none like You. You created the heavens and the Earth. All power is in Your hand. When You speak, universes come to pass. God, I believe You can do what You promised. I'm asking You to bring this dream to pass."

> Don't go your whole life asking God for water when He has living water, something you've never experienced— supernatural favor, supernatural increase, supernatural healing.

Where will you be in ten years if you do as this lady did and start praying bold prayers? God has put things in all of us that we can't accomplish on our own. We may not have the experience, the funds, or the training. The obstacles are too big, and the people coming against us are too strong. If you could do it by yourself, you wouldn't need God's help. This is where you have to pray a bold prayer—not a weak prayer, not a get-by prayer. "God, it's just little ol' me. I'm at a disadvantage, so just give me the leftovers." You have to activate your faith. You have to ask for your dreams, ask for your goals, ask God to open doors that seem impossible. Ask Him to increase your business, ask Him for your children to be mighty in the land, ask Him to take your family to a new level. Yes, it's okay to ask for water, but you're dealing with the One who can give you living water. He has so much more. You may not see how it can happen. That's what faith is all about. "God, I don't see a way, but I know that You have a way."

Don't Be Praying Small

Imagine that there's a huge warehouse in Heaven filled with boxes on shelves. Everywhere you look, it's acres and acres of boxes. Each box has a name on it. When you ask God what the boxes are, He says,

"These boxes are blessings I had for My people, but they never asked for them. There's a business in that box that belonged to Jim, but he never asked. There's a Compaq Center that belonged to Julie, but she didn't ask for it. There's a healing I had for Rolando, there's freedom that belonged to Rachel, and there's a property I had for Maria, but they only prayed for small things. They only asked for water. They never asked Me for their dreams. They never asked Me for something out of the ordinary." Don't let your box stay on a shelf. Don't let those blessings go unclaimed. There are things God has put in your heart, things that He's whispered in the night, but you have to start asking Him for them. Start praying some bold prayers. "Well, what if my desire is not something that God wants?" If it's not the right thing, it's not going to happen. But what if it is the right thing and you never ask? You just prayed small prayers and missed out.

> There are things God has put in your heart, things that He's whispered in the night, but you have to start asking Him for them.

"Joel, I don't want to be greedy. I don't want to be in this just for me." No, your destiny is tied to helping others. Your assignment is tied to building the kingdom. It's not greedy to want to take your family to a new level. It's not wrong to want to see your business blessed so you can support the kingdom in a greater way. The key is, Where is your heart? Of course, if it's just all about you—to look good, to build your ego, without a care about others—that's the wrong motive. But when your heart is to honor God with what He's blessed you with, to bless your family and to be a bigger blessing to others, you can ask for big things and watch what God will do. I have a friend who provides food to a million children a day. He supports the charities that take care of all those kids. That inspires me to pray, "God, bless me in such a way that I can feed a million children." It's going to take bold prayers to do the awesome things God has called you to do. You

> **Start praying big prayers, asking for big things, in order to make a difference in your community, to leave the world a better place.**

haven't seen, heard, or imagined what God has in store for you. Take the limits off Him. Start praying big prayers, asking for big things, in order to make a difference in your community, to leave the world a better place.

It may be that God is going to use you to find a cure for a disease, saving people's lives, or to start a hospital where there is no medical care now. He may want you to develop software that will impact the world, or to write a bestselling book or song that inspires people, or to produce uplifting movies. You may be the one to raise a child who will be the next president, senator, architect, teacher, pastor, or leader. How is this going to happen? By praying bold prayers, by asking God for the dreams He's put in your heart. You have to get in agreement with God. Don't go through life with a small vision. Don't be praying small, thinking small. You activate your faith by not only believing but by asking. You have to say, "God, let me impact the culture. Let my children leave their mark.

> **Pray big, believe big, and God will exceed your expectations.**

Open doors so I can accomplish what You've destined me to do." Pray big, believe big, and God will exceed your expectations. He'll do more than you can imagine.

We're living in a day when God is going to show out in new ways. Number one, He's looking for people who will honor Him by living a life of integrity, of character, keeping Him first place. And number two, He's looking for people who will believe big, people who will get out of their comfort zones and not pray weak prayers, not ask for water, but people who will ask for the living water, for things they cannot do on their own. When you run out of options, that's when God steps in. When the odds are against you, when every circumstance says there's no way, that's when God says, "Let Me show you why I'm called the Great I AM. Let Me show you who controls the universe. Let Me show you how I can open doors, how I can change people's minds, how I can cause the right people to show up, and how I break chains that have held you back. Let Me bring favor, promotion, and influence that catapults you further than you can imagine." We're not dealing with a weak God who's looking for ideas, scratching His head, hoping plans will work out. We're dealing with the most powerful force in the universe. When He calmed the Sea of Galilee, the disciples were in awe. They said, "Who is this man that even the winds and waves obey Him?"

If you want to get God's attention, don't pray weak prayers. God responds to bold prayers. When you pray boldly, you're saying, "God, I know who You are. I recognize that You're all powerful, that nothing can stand against You. What You have purposed will come to pass." People can't stop Him, bad breaks can't stop Him, sickness can't stop Him, how you were raised can't stop Him, and even the wind and waves can't stop Him. You're praying to a God who is in complete control, not just of your life but of your surroundings.

> **If you want to get God's attention, don't pray weak prayers. God responds to bold prayers.**

Dare to Just Ask

In the Scripture, five armies came together against the people of Israel and the people of Gibeon. Joshua had already conquered Jericho and led the Israelites into the Promised Land. Now he was facing another great challenge. The city of Gibeon was next to where he was camped in Gilgal, and the Gibeonites were his allies. They sent word that these armies were attacking them because they had made a treaty of peace with Israel. These kings didn't want the Israelites to be that strong. So Joshua and his men traveled all night, snuck up on the armies, and attacked them. The enemy armies were caught off guard and began to flee. God sent a huge hailstorm and killed many of the enemy soldiers who were fleeing. What's interesting is that not one of Joshua's men was harmed by the hail. As the day was getting late, Joshua was trying to finish them off. He knew that if he didn't completely wipe them out, they would cause trouble in the future. But what could he do? It was about to be dark, and they would escape.

He could have prayed, "God, maybe we can defeat the rest at another time. Just give us strength to get back home and protect us as we travel." That would have been an ordinary prayer. But Joshua wasn't ordinary; he was uncommon. He knew how to pray bold prayers. He stopped what the Israelite soldiers were doing. I can imagine everyone looking at him and someone asking, "Why did you quit chasing them? Why aren't we pursuing them anymore?" Joshua said, "Hang on. I have to pray." They were all intrigued and wondered, *What's he going to pray?* He said, "God, I'm asking You to stop the sun. Keep the moon in its place. God, we need the light to finish them off." I can imagine his men thinking, *The heat's gotten to him. Joshua's losing his mind.* God could have said, "Joshua, what kind of prayer is that? Don't you know that the solar system has to keep moving, that the planets are rotating? Everything is precise. It has to stay perfectly in tune. I can't stop the sun." But God is not intimidated when you pray bold prayers. He's not at a loss to figure out how to bring about His purpose. In fact, He's the One who put the idea in you in the first place.

Joshua asked for the sun to stand still. The next verse simply says,

> God is not intimidated when you pray bold prayers. He's not at a loss to figure out how to bring about His purpose.

"So the sun stood still, and the moon stopped, until the Israelites defeated their enemies." No big explanation is given. You would think there would be several verses describing how this amazing occurrence took place. But it treats it like it's no big deal. God wanted the sun to stop, so it stopped. "Joel, that seems kind of far out." Yes, but we serve a far-out God. It says in Ephesians that God has far-and-beyond favor for us. I know that logically speaking, this doesn't make sense. In the natural, there's no way, but God is supernatural. He created the solar system. He spoke the universe into existence. He can stop what He wants to stop and still cause it to work. Are you praying any bold prayers? Maybe not for the sun to stop, but how about for your child to do something awesome, for you to set a new standard for your family, for you to accomplish the dream that seems far out. God put the thought in you, and perhaps He's just waiting for you to ask.

Don't Miss Your Miracle

A friend of mine wasn't feeling well. He made an appointment with his doctor, and his wife dropped him off at the door. He told her, "Come back in a couple of hours and pick me up." Two hours turned into five months in the hospital. He had COVID-19 and was put on a ventilator. It didn't look good. He finally lost consciousness and was in a coma for seventy-two days. Three times his heart stopped, and they brought him back to life. Once again, the nurse called his wife and said he was about to pass. She went to the hospital, but during the COVID epidemic, visitors were not allowed inside. But at one point, she noticed that the security guard wasn't watching, and she snuck by him and jumped in the elevator. (I'm not suggesting you violate hospital rules; this is her story.) She got off the elevator, waited for the nurses to clear, then went into his room. He was still in a coma.

She called his full name out loud and said, "In the name of Jesus, I command you to come back into this body, to live and not to die." Suddenly, after being in a coma for over two months, he woke up. He told me, "Joel, I heard that prayer." That was the turning point. He began to recover. Today, he's perfectly healthy, fulfilling his purpose. I wonder where he would be if his wife was not that sneaky and if she hadn't known how to pray bold prayers.

My question is, Are you praying any bold prayers? Are you asking God to turn situations around that look impossible, or have you talked yourself out of it? How many miracles are you missing because you're not asking? Dare to ask, not just for your needs, not just for small things, but ask for your dreams, ask for the big things God has put in your heart. He's longing to be good to you. He wants to show you His favor in new ways. He's just waiting for you to ask. If you do this, I believe and declare, as with Joshua, you're going to see supernatural things, doors open that you never dreamed would open, the right people show up, healing, promotion, breakthroughs, and the fullness of your destiny.

> **Are you praying any bold prayers?**

CHAPTER TWO

Blessed Indeed

When you pray bold prayers, when you ask in faith,
declaring God's greatness, He'll make things happen
that you could never make happen.

Most of us believe that we're supposed to be blessed, that God has a good plan for our lives. We ask Him to take care of us, protect us, and provide for our needs. That's good, but God doesn't just want to do the ordinary, the common. He has some uncommon blessings, unusual increase, unprecedented favor for you. His dream for your life is much bigger than your own. But here's the key: If you're going to see the uncommon, you can't just pray common prayers. You can't just ask for the ordinary. You have to ask for dreams that look impossible, for increase that seems out of reach, for favor to overcome obstacles that look too big. If you only pray small prayers, you're going to see small results. If you only ask God to supply your needs, it's going to limit what He will do.

The Scripture says, "You do not have because you do not ask." How many of your prayers are going unanswered because you never asked? You never had the boldness to say, "God, show out in my life. Take me where I can't go on my own. Open this door that looks impossible. Heal me of this sickness that seems permanent. Turn my child around."

Strongholds Broken

I know a lady whose son was way off course for over ten years. He was on drugs, had stolen her credit card and ran up all kinds of debt. He was constantly in and out of jail, causing her heartache and pain. Most people would have prayed an ordinary prayer, such as, "God, just get him off the drugs and help him to stay out of jail." There's nothing wrong with that prayer, but this lady dared to pray a bold prayer. She said, "God, I'm asking You to not only straighten out my son's life but to use him to be a leader, to make a difference with his life." All the circumstances said it would never happen. There was no sign of him improving.

One Sunday morning while this young man was in jail, the inmates were watching our television program. He hadn't planned to watch the broadcast, but when he heard me talking about how God has a plan for your life and how nothing that you've done has to keep you from your destiny, something came alive inside. Strongholds in his mind were broken. Some weeks later, he was able to come to our service at Lakewood, stood up and gave his life to Christ. I met him afterward in the lobby. While he looked very rough, with tattoos, piercings, and a long beard, he had tears running down his cheeks. He told how his mother had been praying for him for years and how he felt a love and sense of purpose that he had never felt. Today, he's the pastor of a church and is helping other people who are going through what he went through. His mother is so thrilled, so grateful to God. But I wonder where her son would be if she had prayed a weak prayer, a get-by prayer. "God, just don't let him get harmed." Maybe he wouldn't be free

> I wonder where her son would be if she had prayed a weak prayer, a get-by prayer.

and making such a difference. Pray bold prayers over your children, over your finances, over your dreams.

I pray every day, "God, take our ministry where no ministry has ever gone." You may say, "Joel, isn't that kind of selfish, kind of arrogant, kind of greedy?" No, that's releasing your faith. That's what's going to take you to the fullness of your destiny. We've seen God open doors that have never opened for other ministries. Television networks that have a nonreligious policy, that have never aired inspirational programming, now air our program every week. They break their own rules to put us on. That's what happens when you pray bold prayers. I pray every day, "God, let my children go further than I've ever gone, let them supersede anything that I've done. Let them impact the culture in a greater way." Don't let that prayer go unanswered because you never prayed it for your children, because you never asked God to do the unusual, the uncommon.

Open Your Mouth Wide

In Psalm 81, God says, "Open your mouth wide, and I will fill it with good things." The principle is that how wide your mouth is open is how much God is going to fill. If you have a wide mouth, if you're praying bold prayers, asking Him to do things that seem impossible, you're going to see Him show out in your life. But if your mouth is barely open, if you're just asking God to meet your needs, just believing to get through the day and content to settle where you are, you're going to see His goodness in a limited way. My point is not to discount the small things God does. I thank Him that He wakes me up in the morning and gives me breath to breathe. I'm grateful that He's supplying my needs. But I'm saying to not stop there. Open your

> **Open your mouth wide, ask Him for your dreams.**

mouth wide, ask Him for your dreams, ask Him to give you that business, ask Him to build that children's home, ask Him to free you from that sickness. This is one time where it's good to have a big mouth. It's good to ask for things that seem unlikely. God calls those healthy prayers.

A young lady came forward during one of our church services and asked if I would pray that she would make a C on her final math exam. That struck me as odd. I asked, "Why would we pray for a C and not an A?" She said, "I'm not good at math, and I've never made an A. I just want to pass." I didn't tell her, but I wanted to say, "That's a sick prayer. That prayer has the flu. That prayer is depressed." I wonder what prayers are not being answered for you, not because God won't do it or because it's too hard, but because you never asked. You never had the boldness to open your mouth wide and ask for what you really want rather than what you thought would happen.

If you're single, don't think it's a sign of humility to just ask to meet anyone. "God, they don't have to be attractive, or have a good job, or to be talented. I just want someone who's breathing." You better cancel that prayer right now. Your next prayer will be, "God, get them out of my life." If God answered what you're praying for, is it

> **If God answered what you're praying for, is it what you *really* want?**

what you *really* want? What if God has someone awesome on the way for you, someone better than you could imagine, but God says to the angel, "Hold off on that awesome person I was about to send. Go ahead and send that person who's content with being mediocre. They're okay with it." Now, I realize that's not how God operates, but you need to ask God for what you really want, not a watered-down version, not an "I don't deserve much. Just let me get by" prayer. Ask Him for someone awesome, someone tall, handsome, well-off, smart, good-looking, funny, and talented. That's what Victoria did. God answered her prayer.

My question is, How wide open is your mouth? Are you asking God to just do the ordinary, to just help you get by, to just meet your needs? God is saying, "Open your mouth wider and watch what I'll do." I told the young lady that I didn't want to pray for a C, but I was going to pray for an A. Her eyes got real big. I said, "You were created to excel. You have talent in you that you haven't tapped into. Quit telling yourself you can only make a C, and start thanking God that you're going to make an A." She went home with a new perspective. She started opening her mouth wider. She studied, she prepared, and about a month later she came back and said that for the first time she had made an A in math. Even her teacher said, "You really surprised me." That would never have happened if she hadn't had the boldness to ask for what she really wanted.

If you break out of the rut and start praying bold prayers, you're going to have some of these first times. For the first time, you're not struggling to get by; you have overflow. For the first time, you're not fighting the addiction; you're totally free. For the first time, there's somebody awesome in your life to love. For the first time, you're living your dream, doing more than you ever imagined. Now do your part. Stop asking for a C, and start asking for an A. You're not inconveniencing God by asking big. It's not as though somebody else will be left out if He does what you want. You're not being greedy or selfish. No, God has unlimited favor, unlimited power. His being good to you doesn't stop Him from being good to someone else. The Scripture says, "It

> If you break out of the rut and start praying bold prayers, you're going to have some of these first times.

> "It is the Father's good pleasure to give you the kingdom." Maybe He's just waiting for you to ask.

is the Father's good pleasure to give you the kingdom." Maybe He's just waiting for you to ask.

"Bless Me Indeed"

In 1 Chronicles 4 is a family genealogy that lists some of the people of Judah. It's one person who descended from another, one name after another for forty-four names. Reading them, it gets a bit boring. Then at the forty-fifth name, instead of just listing this one and going on to the over one hundred names to come, the writer pauses and gives a brief description. It's as if to say that this next man did something significant. He didn't just live and die and get his name in the family line, but he stood out. He did something worth pausing for. He left his mark. It says, "There was a man named Jabez who was more honorable than any of his brothers. His mother named him this because his birth had been so painful." Jabez stood out because he honored God in a great way. He lived a life of excellence and integrity, but that wasn't the only reason.

The name Jabez means "sorrow, pain, trouble." In those days, names were given much like prophecies. They predicted what would happen. The name Joshua means "savior." Every time someone said, "Hello, Joshua," courage must have filled his heart. He went on to lead the Israelites into the Promised Land. The name Jacob means "deceiver." He lived a life deceiving people, just as he was named. Think about how Jabez must have felt. His mother declared over him that his life would be full of heartache, pain, and trouble. Every time someone said, "Hey, Jabez," they were reminding him that he was at a disadvantage, that he'd had bad breaks, a rough start. You would think if anyone's name would be mentioned in the genealogy and then passed right over, it would be his.

But despite the odds being against Jabez, despite what his mother had prophesied over him, he prayed a prayer that changed the course of his life. He said, "God, I'm asking You to bless me indeed." It's one thing if he had just asked God to bless him, but when he said "indeed," he was saying, "God, bless me in abundance, bless me with overflow, bless me with so much favor that I can leave my mark." I've read that saying "indeed" was like adding five exclamation points. He was saying, "God, do something extraordinary, uncommon, unusual." Against all odds, somehow Jabez had the nerve to open his mouth wide. He went on to say, "And enlarge my territory, expand my borders." Think of the boldness that took. Every circumstance said he was limited. If he had accepted it, he would have been just another name on the list. But the Scripture goes on to say, "And God granted him his request."

> **Saying "indeed" was like adding five exclamation points.**

Jabez didn't raise his rod and part the Red Sea as Moses did. He didn't kill a giant as David did. He didn't save the Israelites as Esther did. He doesn't have chapters of the Bible dedicated to telling his story. But because he prayed a bold prayer, because he said, "God bless me indeed," God paused the scripture and said, "Wait a minute. Don't just pass by this man. Don't just list his name and move on. I need to say something about him. He was unusual. He didn't let the circumstances determine his destiny. He didn't stay with the status quo. He dared to ask Me for the uncommon."

Do as Jabez did and say, "God, bless me indeed. Not a little blessing, not just enough to get by and meet my needs, but bless me with overflow, bless me with more than enough, take me where I can't go on my own." Then in the years to come, when someone is reading your family line, you won't just be a name on a list. They'll have to pause and say, "Wow! They were a difference maker. They left our family better than it was, set new standards, and took us to a new level." You're not supposed to live and die and nobody remembers you were here. The number one way to leave your mark is to live honorably before God, stay on the high road, don't give in to temptation and compromise. The number two way is to dare to say, "God, bless me indeed." Have a big vision and believe for what seems impossible. Don't be limited by how you were raised, what was passed down, or by how unlikely your dream looks.

I'm sure that the people who are listed before and after Jabez in this genealogy were good people and accomplished things. Some of them must have prayed, must have asked God for things, but nothing is mentioned about them. It's significant that God paused to tell us that Jabez said, "Bless me indeed." I wonder what would happen if we were to start every day praying, "God, bless me indeed. Enlarge my territories, give me more influence, more resources, more opportunity." Don't do it just once a month, but when you wake up every morning, say, "Lord, bless me indeed today." At the office, under your breath, say, "God, bless me indeed." Before you go to bed, close the day by saying, "Father, thank You for blessing me indeed."

> I wonder what would happen if we were to start every day praying, "God, bless me indeed. Enlarge my territories, give me more influence, more resources, more opportunity."

A Double Portion

God wants you to tap into His favor, to see the surpassing greatness of His power. That takes bold prayers. That takes people who take the limits off God, people who won't be moved by how impossible their dream looks. Maybe you've been praying for God to bless you. That's good, but I'm asking you to put the "indeed" on it. "God, bless me in unusual ways. Do something uncommon, out of the ordinary. Show me something that I've never seen. I'm asking You for unprecedented favor."

In the Scripture, Elisha served the prophet Elijah for many years. He was faithful to take care of Elijah and go everywhere he went. When Elijah was about to be taken to Heaven, he asked Elisha what he wanted. You would think that Elisha would ask for something ordinary. He might have asked for Elijah's staff or to be given a monetary gift, funding for a 401(k) plan. But Elisha understood this principle of how to pray bold prayers. He said, "Elijah, I want a double portion of your spirit." He was saying, "I want to do twice as many miracles as you. I want to have twice the anointing, twice the favor, twice the influence, twice the resources." He was asking God to bless him indeed. Elijah could have responded, "You have a lot of nerve. You sure are greedy. You need to think again and ask for something more common, more ordinary." No, Elijah liked his boldness. He said, in effect, "You keep serving me and you will have exactly what you asked."

Not long after that, Elijah was caught up in a whirlwind and taken to Heaven. Just as God promised, Elisha received a double portion of his spirit. He performed twice as many miracles as Elijah. That wouldn't have happened if he had not said, "God, bless me indeed." The "indeed" is to fulfill your destiny. The "indeed" is to go places that you can't go on your own. You may be doing fine where you are. God has blessed you. That's great, but that's not your final destination. God has bigger things, greater opportunities, more influence. Don't get stuck because you're not asking.

Don't get stuck because you're not asking.

The Scripture says, "Elijah was human, as we are, and yet when he prayed that it would not rain, no rain fell for three and a half years." Sometimes we think of the people in the Bible as superhuman. We think they had so much more faith than us, and God must have favored them because they were so special. But this scripture starts off saying, "Elijah was human." Of course, we know he was human. He wasn't an alien. God was saying this to let us know that Elijah was an ordinary person just like you and me, who was filled with the Spirit of the Most High God. He didn't necessarily feel special. He didn't walk around with a supernatural glow. The reason we're talking about Elijah is that he dared to pray bold prayers. He dared to ask for the impossible. That's what made him stand out. "Well, Joel, I'm not a minister. I'm not in leadership. I don't have a lot of influence." You're right where Elijah was. Quit discounting yourself. Quit thinking that you can't pray for something big, that you don't have the faith, you don't come from the right family. The requirement is, Are you a human? Since you are, God says you can ask for things that seem impossible.

Now start opening your mouth wide, and God will fill it. Every day say, "Lord, bless me indeed." Don't just pray "bless me"; add the "indeed." Put the exclamation point on it. That's saying, "God, bless me with abundance, give me overflow, and show out in my life." If you do this, I believe and declare that like God did with Jabez, He's about to enlarge your territories. He's about to bless you indeed with unusual favor, with uncommon opportunities, with a future that you've never imagined.

CHAPTER THREE

Supernatural Provision

Our God is not limited by what you don't have, and He knows exactly what you need, when you need it, and how to get it to you.

When we look at our circumstances, sometimes we don't see how we can get ahead. How can we accomplish our dreams? How can we own and not just rent? How can we leave an inheritance to our grandchildren like the Scripture says? In the natural, with inflation, gas and food costing more, we may not see a way. But God is a supernatural God. When we come to the end of our resources, He steps in and says, "I'll make streams in the desert. I'll take five loaves and two fish and multiply them to feed thousands." When Peter didn't have money to pay his taxes, Jesus told him to go to the lake and the first fish he caught would have a large silver coin in its mouth, enough to pay his and Jesus' taxes. God was showing us that He has supernatural provision. He's not limited by what you don't have. He's not limited by how you were raised or the family you come from. There may be lack, struggle, barely getting by. That's how it's been, but you've been raised up to break that negative cycle. You're the one who's going to come out of not enough into more than enough. God is not a get-by God. He's an overflow God. Don't live with a lack mentality, a not-enough, limited mindset. Have an abundant mentality. "I will lend and not borrow. My cup runs over. Because I honor God, I live under the open windows of Heaven, with blessings that I cannot contain."

You have to prosper in your mind before you prosper in your circumstances. You have to give God permission to bless you. Are you in agreement with what He wants to do, or are you thinking you're stuck? *I've never seen prices this high. I don't see how I can ever get out of this neighborhood. The stock market has me worried.* You're looking at everything in the natural.

> You have to prosper in your mind before you prosper in your circumstances.

You have to realize that God is supernatural. The good news is, He's not having a down year. He's not scratching His head, thinking, *I didn't see inflation coming. It's too bad that the price of houses just keeps going up. A lot of businesses aren't going to make it.* No, God owns it all. He makes streets of gold. You are connected to a supply line that will never run dry. The economy may go up or down, but that's not your source; God is your source. We're grateful for our jobs, grateful for employment and a good boss. But God is not dependent on those things or people. He has provision in your future that is beyond your normal salary, beyond your training, beyond your experience. He's not looking at what people look at— people's qualifications and talents. He's looking at your heart. He sees how faithful you are, how you always keep Him first place, how you have a desire to help others and build the kingdom. He sees you have a dream to accomplish what seems over your head, and He hears the boldness in your prayers. That's when God will step in and show you supernatural provision. He'll open doors you never dreamed would open. He'll bring income, resources, and contracts that will thrust you further than you've ever imagined.

"Joel, this sounds good but my boss doesn't give me any credit. My bills are outpacing my income. I take one step forward, then two steps back. I don't think I'll ever have abundance." Let me give you a key: If you have a poor mouth, you're going to have a poor life. God wants to show you supernatural increase, but you can cancel it out with a negative tongue. Your words can speak death or they can speak life. You can speak lack or you can speak abundance. You can speak not enough or you can speak more than enough. Psalm 35 says, "Let them continually say, 'Let the Lord be magnified, who takes pleasure in the prosperity of His children.'" They were supposed to go around continually saying, "God takes pleasure in prospering me." God knew if they started talking negatively, talking lack and not enough, they would have a limited mindset. They would never see the blessing, the favor, or the abundance that He had in store. Every time you're tempted to talk about what you don't have, how you can't accomplish the dream, turn it around. "Father, thank You that You take pleasure in prospering me. I may not see how, but I know that You have supernatural provision, supernatural increase. You're not limited by what limits me."

> If you have a poor mouth, you're going to have a poor life. God wants to show you supernatural increase, but you can cancel it out with a negative tongue.

Put God First

In Luke 5, Jesus was at the Sea of Galilee. There were so many people crowded around to hear His teaching that He asked Peter if He could borrow his fishing boat. Peter agreed and pushed out from the shore. When Jesus was finished teaching, He told Peter to launch out into the deep and he would catch a great haul of fish. Peter had fished all night and caught nothing. He was a professional fisherman who

knew when and where to fish. Jesus was a teacher, a rabbi. I'm sure
Peter thought, *Who is this man to tell me how to fish? He should stick to
teaching, and I'll stick to fishing.* He said, in effect, "Jesus, this doesn't
make sense to me. Nevertheless, at Your word, I'm going to do it."
He let his nets down and caught so many fish that the nets began
to tear. He had to call his partners in another boat to help, and both
boats became so loaded down that they
were about to sink. What's interesting is

> **He knows where your provision is, and He knows how to get it to you.**

that there were no fish there a few hours
before, but God controls the fish. He
knows where your provision is, and He
knows how to get it to you. It may not
make sense or be logical or what you
were expecting. God likes to do things out of the ordinary, uncommon, so you'll know it is from His hand.

Peter let Jesus borrow his boat. That was his business, his source
of income. He could have said, "Jesus, I'm busy. I'm too tired. I don't
know You. Go find another boat." But he gave his resource to Jesus.
He was generous. This was symbolic of putting God first place. Proverbs says, "Honor the Lord with your income and the firstfruits of all
your crops. Then He will fill your barns with abundance and your
vats will overflow." If you're going to see supernatural provision, you
have to be a giver. Honor God with your firstfruits, the first part of
your income. Invite Him into your business. If you work forty hours
a week, give Him your firstfruits. "God, You can use my boat these
first four hours. I'm giving You this income." When you let God use
your boat, you're setting yourself up for overflow, for abundance. We
think the opposite. *If I give, I'm going to have less.* No, that's a seed
you're sowing. You can't give God something without Him giving you
more back in return. Peter owned the boat, but God owns the sea. He
controls the universe. When you let God use your boat, He'll cause
the fish to find you. He'll cause contracts, opportunities, and good

breaks to track you down. The Scripture says, "Give, and it will be given to you, but not in the same measure—pressed down, shaken together, and running over." That's the way our God is. He's a net-breaking God.

> When you let God use your boat, He'll cause the fish to find you.

It's significant that when Peter let Jesus use his boat, he had just fished all night and caught nothing. His mindset was lack, scarcity, not enough. Jesus was about to choose Peter to become His first disciple. He could have just thanked Peter for letting Him use the boat and said, "I want you to be My disciple." But Jesus didn't want Peter to have a limited mindset associated with Him. So He told him to go back into the deep, and he caught so many fish that his nets began to break. When Peter came back to the shore, Jesus said, "Peter, from now on you're going to become a fisher of men." Now Peter's mindset was abundance, overflow, more than enough. That's the mentality Jesus wanted him to have—not a fisher of men who barely gets by, never catches anything, and can't accomplish his dream. No, we have to have a different mindset. You may have seasons where you catch nothing, but that is not your destiny. Abundance is coming. God has some net-breaking blessings in your future. You couldn't make it happen. You fished all night and caught nothing. You did your best, worked hard, honored God, but you still came up empty. Your time is coming. God is directing those fish right now. He's lining up supernatural provision. He's

> God has some net-breaking blessings in your future.

bringing something you've never seen, boat-sinking blessings, increase that not only affects you but spills over to your children and grandchildren. You're going to have to call some other boats to take in the overflow. David says, "My cup runs over." God is going to bless you to where future generations will get the runover. Your family line will be blessed because you honored God and had an abundant mentality. God entrusted you with net-breaking blessings.

Net-Breaking Blessings

I talked to a woman who works part-time in commercial real estate. Her main focus is raising her children. She also volunteers faithfully at her church. A friend of hers, a high-powered businessman, wanted to sell a large piece of property that borders on a freeway. He could have called his attorney to sell it or hired a leading real estate company. Instead, he called this woman and listed it with her. He wasn't in a hurry to sell, and the property sat on the market year after year. She kept raising the price, from several million dollars to twelve million to over twenty million. People told her that the property would never sell for that much, that she was wasting her time. Not long ago, a large global company wanted to purchase the property. She thought her friend would want to bring in his legal team to lead the negotiations, but he said, "No, you're in charge."

Although she wasn't skilled in negotiating large contracts, she said, "When I went into the meeting, I felt a boldness, a confidence. I knew the favor of God was on my life." She stood firm, wouldn't back down on the price she wanted for the property. After two days, they said, "We know the value is not this high, but something just feels right. We're going to purchase it." The commission from that one good break will spill over to her children and grandchildren. She said, "Joel, I never dreamed that God would bless me in such a way." God has some of these net-breaking blessings for you. He has supernatural provision, supernatural increase. He's not limited by your education, your experience, who you know, or how you were raised. God knows how to bring the fish. You do your part and let Him into your boat.

Honor Him with your income, and God will bless you in ways you've never imagined.

When Peter saw how many fish were in his nets, the Scripture says, "He was awestruck at the size of his catch." God

> **God knows how to bring the fish. You do your part and let Him into your boat.**

is going to do some things that leave you awestruck. You thought you'd be paying off your house for thirty years, then suddenly a net-breaking blessing comes—a contract, a good break, an inheritance—and you're into overflow. You thought you'd always be stuck in that neighborhood or environment, then suddenly a new door opened, a promotion you weren't next in line for. The fish came looking for you. "Well, Joel, this is encouraging, but I don't see how it can happen." You don't have to see how. Leave the how up to God. Just believe that it will happen. We can't see the how because we're in the natural, but God is supernatural. We're limited, but God is unlimited. If you get stuck on the how, you'll talk yourself out of it. Your mind will come up with a thousand reasons why it's not going to happen. God's ways are not our ways. He has ways you've never thought of.

Water Out of a Rock

After God delivered the two million Israelites from slavery in Egypt and parted the Red Sea, the people were in the desert headed toward the Promised Land. There were no grocery stores out there, no fast food, no DoorDash, and there was no water. They began to complain, "Moses, why did you bring us out here to die of thirst and hunger?" God didn't go to all that trouble to bring them out of slavery, to free them from Pharaoh, and then let them starve to death. God will allow situations where it looks impossible so He can show us His supernatural provision. Don't be surprised if you face times when all the facts say, "There's no way. Your resources are limited. You fished all night and caught nothing." No, God is up to something. He didn't bring you this far to leave you.

God told Moses to take his staff and strike a rock in the desert. When he did, water started pouring out of the rock. Supernatural provision. God can make things happen that defy the odds, things that you couldn't plan for. You have to trust Him. Everything in your mind will tell you, *You'll never have abundance. You'll always be thirsty. You'll always struggle, have debt, not enough.* Logically speaking, that may be true. But God will defy logic. He knows how to bring water out of a rock. The Scripture says, "He makes streams in the barren places, rivers in the desert." There may be some barren places in your life. You don't see how it could ever change. No, get ready. God is about to strike the rock. You're going to see provision you can't explain, good breaks that don't make sense, increase that's not logical. The same God who brought water out of a rock can cause promotion to find you, the right people to track you down, and abundance to come knocking on your door.

> The same God who brought water out of a rock can cause promotion to find you, the right people to track you down, and abundance to come knocking on your door.

If we could do this in our own strength, we wouldn't need God. He will put dreams in your heart that you can't accomplish by yourself. You don't have the resources, the funds, or the connections. It's easy to get discouraged and let what we see in the natural talk us out of it. This is where you have to stir up your faith and pray a bold prayer: "God, I believe that You have supernatural provision. I believe that You have net-breaking blessings, that You can still bring water out of a rock."

Rams Are in Your Future

I know a couple who were believing to have children for a long time with no success. After much prayer and fertility treatment, she became pregnant with triplets. They were so excited, but during the pregnancy, there were complications. The babies were born prematurely, weighing less than a pound each. They had to stay in a neonatal intensive care unit for six months. By the grace of God, the babies grew, and today they're perfectly healthy. The parents had insurance, but it didn't cover everything. A few months after they brought their children home, they received a bill for two million dollars. The father was a police officer, and the mother was an educator. In the natural, they would be paying on that bill the rest of their lives. They would always be in debt. But God knows how to bring water out of a rock. He knows how to cause fish to find you. They didn't start complaining. They didn't get discouraged. They kept thanking God for supernatural provision and declaring what He promised. "We will lend and not borrow. Father, thank You that our cup runs over, that we have more than enough, that You take pleasure in prospering us." If you're going to see God's blessings, you have to have this abundant mentality. You have to know that He is Jehovah Jireh, the Lord your provider.

> If you're going to see God's blessings, you have to have this abundant mentality. You have to know that He is Jehovah Jireh, the Lord your provider.

The name "Jehovah Jireh" comes from Genesis 22, when Abraham was about to sacrifice his son Isaac on Mount Moriah as a test of his obedience to God. Right before he went through with it, an angel told him to stop. But Abraham still needed an animal to sacrifice. He heard this noise in the brush and saw a ram caught in the thicket, which became the sacrifice. "Abraham named that place Jehovah Jireh, the Lord will provide." What's interesting is that rams aren't normally found that high up on the mountains, but God knows how to get the provision to you. The ram was waiting on Abraham. It was going up the mountain before Abraham even knew he needed it. It was already en route. God has some rams waiting for you. He's already lined up your provision, your abundance. Before you had the setback, He put the ram in place. Maybe you grew up in a family of lack and struggle. Don't worry. Rams are in your future. It may look as though you're stuck. You don't have the funding for your dream. How can you expand your business? Stay encouraged. A ram will be waiting for you. Jehovah Jireh, the Lord your provider, has already put abundance, good breaks, and supernatural provision in your path.

That's why we can stay in peace. He's the Lord our provider. Our job is not our provider, our boss is not our provider, and our salary is not our provider. Our provider is the God who spoke worlds into existence, the God who makes streets of gold, the God who causes fish to show up, the God who brings water out of a rock. He's the God who puts a ram in a thicket, the God who says you'll lend and not borrow, the God who says your cup will run over. That's who is ordering your steps. That's who has planned out your future. You may know Him as your Savior. That's the most important. You may know Him as your healer. That's good. But you need to know Him as your provider as well. He has supernatural provision.

> Our job is not our provider, our boss is not our provider, and our salary is not our provider. Our provider is the God who spoke worlds into existence.

The couple with triplets didn't see how it could work out, but they kept standing in faith, believing that God would make a way. Right before Christmas that year, the hospital called and said, "We've never done this, but we've decided to cancel your two-million-dollar debt."

Like Peter, they were awestruck. They didn't see that coming. Like with Abraham, that was a ram waiting for them. You don't know what God has waiting for you. It's hidden right now. You can't see it yet. But at the right time, it's going to show up. It's not going to be ordinary, something you were expecting. It's going to leave you awestruck. It's going to be net-breaking blessings, abundance that runs over to your children, increase that takes you from just enough to more than enough.

When You Honor God

In 2013, a young mother, who is a registered nurse, and her husband were pregnant with another child. Unfortunately, the baby son was born without proper brain function. Six months later, he passed. The baby's mother was so distraught, so empty, that she didn't feel as though she had any purpose. She wasn't raised in church and didn't have a faith background. But in that dark time, she found the missing link was to have a connection to God. She decided to get to know God on a personal level, got involved in a good church, started volunteering, and things started to change. To try to distract herself from the pain of the loss, she started researching hair products for black women, experimenting with different things that worked for her. She put her discoveries on her Instagram and shared tips on taking care of your hair and ways to style it. She thought maybe one day she'd open a hair salon. Much to her surprise, her Instagram blew up. There was so much interest in her hair products that she decided to start selling them online.

She began in her kitchen, and the business grew and grew. They moved to the garage, then over the next few years, it took off and became a multimillion dollar business. In 2023, Procter & Gamble purchased her company for an amount she never dreamed, with her and her husband remaining CEO and COO of the brand. On top of that, they committed ten million dollars to her charity to help educate children living in communities vulnerable to poverty as well as provide education and economic opportunities in those same communities. You don't know what kind of rams God has waiting for you. When you honor Him, when you live with an abundant mentality, He'll do things you didn't see coming. He'll not just meet your needs, He'll provide supernatural provision. He'll provide uncommon, unusual things that you can't explain.

This woman told me that she didn't feel qualified to run a company that large. She had never been to business school and was trained in health care. Some of her friends told her she was making a mistake leaving her nursing job. But God has things in your future that are not going to make sense to everyone. Water out of a rock doesn't make sense. Telling Peter to go back and drop his nets into the deep where there had been no fish a few hours before made no sense. Yet there's a net-breaking blessing. Don't let people talk you out of what God put in your heart. His ways are not our ways. The blessing is in the obedience. The ram is waiting for you where God told you to go.

> God has things in your future that are not going to make sense to everyone. Water out of a rock doesn't make sense.

A Shift Is Coming

After the two million Israelites escaped from slavery in Egypt, every morning God provided them with manna, something like bread, on the ground in the desert. That's how they survived. But in Numbers 11, the people got tired of it and complained to Moses, "We want some meat to eat. Back in Egypt, we had fish and steaks. Now all we have is this dried-up bread." God didn't like their complaining, but He is so merciful that the Scripture says, "God shifted the wind and caused hundreds of thousands of quail to come in from the sea." With that one shift, two million people had steak dinners for a whole month. In response to Moses thinking this was a complete impossibility, God was saying, "Is there any limit to My power? Don't you realize that I control the universe? I put rams in a bush. I tell fish to get in a net. I tell water to come out of a rock. I tell Compaq Centers to go to My people." They were awestruck at what God had done.

We're praying about paying our light bill, but look at how God thinks—abundance, overflow, more than enough. As with them, God is about to shift some things in your life. He's going to cause the quail to come looking for you. You couldn't have made it happen. You didn't have the connections, the experience, or the background. But you've kept God first place. You've been faithful. You've honored Him with your firstfruits. Now He is going to cause the winds to blow in your direction. A shift is coming, from borrowing to lending. A shift is coming, from renting to owning. A shift is coming, from employee to employer. A shift is coming, from not enough to more than enough.

You may not see how this can happen. Your mind is telling you, *There's no way. How could you get out of debt? How could you leave your family better? How could you accomplish your dream?* God is asking you what He asked Moses: "Is there anything too hard for Me?" You're looking at it in the natural, but God has supernatural provision. One shift and you'll go from no fish to a net-breaking blessing. You'll go from experimenting with hair products to a business exploding. You'll go from a

> God is asking you what He asked Moses: "Is there anything too hard for Me?"

two-million-dollar medical bill to being debt-free. Are you looking at how big the lack, the debt, the struggle is, or how big your God is? Have a new perspective and say, "Let God be magnified, who takes pleasure in prospering me." Get in agreement with God. Have an abundant mentality. He has some rams waiting for you. He's already lined up some net-breaking blessings. If you do this, I believe and declare that you're going to see supernatural provision. Doors will suddenly open. Good breaks and opportunities will find you. You're going to be awestruck at the goodness of God.

CHAPTER FOUR

Awaken Your Great Faith

Dare to ask for something that causes God to be amazed. Dare to believe for something that will cause God to marvel.

We all face dreams that seem too big, obstacles that are too much to overcome. The house loan didn't go through, the car broke down and took all the money we'd saved for a vacation, or the stress at work just keeps getting stronger. It's easy to get discouraged and settle where we are. But God wouldn't have put the dream in your heart if He didn't have a way to bring it to pass. He wouldn't have let you get into that challenge if He weren't planning on bringing you out. But our faith, what we believe, will have a great impact on what's going to happen. It's not just up to God. He has all the power in the world. It's up to us. He works through faith. If you believe little, you will receive little. If you think small, talk small, pray small, and say, "I've reached my limits," you'll get stuck where you are.

The Scripture talks about different levels of faith. In Matthew 8, the disciples and Jesus were in a boat when a huge storm arose. The disciples started looking at the winds and how big the waves were. They were frightened and woke Jesus up, saying, "Lord, save us! We're about to die!" Before Jesus calmed the storm, before He spoke to the waves, He looked at them and said, "Why do you have such little faith?" He

> ## "Why do you have such little faith?"

was saying, "You've seen what I can do. You've seen Me heal the sick, multiply the fish and loaves, restore the broken. Why are you still stuck at that low level of faith when you know I can do anything?"

The apostle Paul also talks about people "whose faith is weak." He is referring to people who barely believe, who get talked out of their dreams, who at any moment will give up on what God put in their heart. But there are also two places in Scripture where Jesus talks about people with "great faith." These were people who dared to believe despite the circumstances. They knew that our God is all-powerful, that He can make streams in the desert, that He can open doors no person can shut, that He can do what medicine cannot do.

If you're going to reach the fullness of your destiny, it's not going to happen with a weak faith, little faith, doubting faith, average faith. It's going to take great faith. The good news is, it's in you. You have the ability to go places you've never gone, to overcome challenges that seem too big, but here's the key: You have to awaken your great faith. You have to stir up what God put in you. The enemy would love for you to go through life with little faith, a weak faith, not believing, full of doubt. He would love for you to be comfortable where you are, not stretching, not putting a demand on your faith. But in the days we're living in, average faith is not going to cut it. To overcome forces that are trying to stop you, you can't have ordinary faith. To leave your mark, you can't just believe like everyone else. It's going

> ## In the days we're living in, average faith is not going to cut it.

to take people who will dare to believe big, to pray big, to take the limits off. You have to say, "God, I don't see a way, but I know that You have a way." God wants to do something new in your life, something uncommon, out of the ordinary, but if you're going to see great favor, you have to have great faith.

Prophesy to the Dead Bones

Great faith is already in you. I'm just trying to awaken your great faith. That's how you're going to go to a new level. That's how your business will take off, how you're going to break the addiction, how your children are going to get back on course. It's not just going to be by your willpower, your strength, or your intellect. Those are all good, but it's going to happen because of your faith. When you get in agreement with God, angels go to work, forces of darkness are broken, good breaks start chasing you down. Great faith activates great favor. What you believe is setting limits for your life. Don't go around with a weak faith, little faith, doubting faith, complaining faith. Get out of your box. Start believing for bigger things. It's not that God is limited. He's all-powerful, but we can limit Him by our small thinking, by our small prayers.

> **What you believe is setting limits for your life.**

In the Scripture, the prophet Ezekiel saw a vision of a valley that was filled with dry bones. It was like a huge graveyard with thousands of bones scattered on the ground. These bones represented what was dead—dreams that didn't work out, disappointments, closed doors. God was about to bring these bones together and cause these people to come back to life. But before any of this happened, before God did the miraculous, He asked Ezekiel, "Do you believe that these dead bones can live?" He was saying, "Ezekiel, what is your level of faith? Do you have a weak faith, little faith, doubting faith, or do you have great faith? Do you believe that I can do the impossible?" Ezekiel answered, "Oh, Sovereign Lord." He was saying, "God, You control the universe. You parted the Red Sea. You stopped the sun for Joshua. You gave Sarah a baby at the age of ninety. Yes, this looks impossible, but I know that You can do the impossible." God said, in effect,

"Ezekiel, that's what I'm looking for. I'm not looking for someone with a weak faith, or a complainer, or someone who's going to tell Me all the reasons it's not going to happen. I'm looking for great faith." He told Ezekiel to prophesy to those dead bones. When he did, the bones began to come together, muscles and organs appeared, skin formed over them, and God breathed His breath over them. It looked like something in a movie when those people came back to life and stood up.

Like Ezekiel, great faith is in you. It's not in your mind or your intellect; it's in your spirit. For some people, it's been asleep a long time. God is about to bring dead things in you back to life, but there is one requirement that He's looking for—great faith. The good news is, you have it. Now do your part and get in agreement with God. "Father, thank You that I will accomplish my dreams. I believe I will get well. I believe this will be a bountiful year. Lord, thank You that You're breathing on my life right now." You keep that attitude of faith and watch what God will do. Great faith brings great favor.

> **Great faith brings great favor.**

"According to Your Faith"

When a friend of mine's daughter was three years old, a very heavy piece of iron fell on two of her fingers and cut the tips off. They rushed her to the emergency room. After taking X-rays and doing all the tests, the specialist came in and said to the father, "I'm sorry, but there's nothing we can do to restore her fingers to normal. She'll never have nails on those two fingers, and the fingers will always be a little bit shorter." The bone had been cut, and all they could do was a skin graft to hopefully make them look as smooth as possible. The father was very respectful, but he said to the doctor, "I believe that God can restore my little girl's fingers and make them normal again." The doctor looked at him strangely. He was from another country and did not come from a faith background. He said, "That's fine, if you want to believe that, but you have to understand that the bones are missing. Neither finger will ever be the right length, and there's no way she's going to have fingernails." When the father's wife came in, the doctor took her aside and said, "Your husband is in shock. He won't accept the fact that the tip of those fingers have been cut off."

They did the skin graft. Six weeks later, they brought the little girl back for a checkup. When the doctor took the bandage off, his first words were, "Oh my God!" The father was alarmed and said, "What's wrong?" The doctor replied, "The finger-nails have grown back, and it looks like the fingers are the exact right length." That was over twenty years ago, and her fingers still look perfectly normal to this day. My point is not to say we should deny reality, but I am saying that God has the final say. There are natural laws, but God is supernatural. He's not limited by what limits us. When we believe, when we pray, all things are possible. When you have great faith, you will see the greatness of our God.

> **There are natural laws, but God is supernatural. He's not limited by what limits us.**

Jesus healed a blind man and said, "According to your faith let it be to you." The man wasn't healed according to God's faith but according to his own faith. To get where God wants to take you is going to take more than average faith. The amazing future He has in store, the doors He's going to open, and the favor you're going to see won't happen with ordinary faith. There will be dreams that are way too big for you. There will be Goliaths of opposition where you don't stand a chance. There will be times when you're in way over your head. That's when you have to be an Ezekiel and say, "God, I know these dead bones can live. I know that You can defeat these enemies. I know that Your favor on my life will take me where I can't go on my own."

At the end of a parable that Jesus told in Luke 18, He asked this question: "When I return, what kind of faith will I find on the Earth?" If God showed up at your house, what kind of faith would He find? Small faith? Weak faith? Complaining faith? Awaken your great faith. You don't have to figure out how it's going to happen. All you have to do is believe.

> **If God showed up at your house, what kind of faith would He find?**

Believe for What Causes God to Marvel

In Luke 7 is the story of a Roman centurion, meaning that he had a hundred men under his command officer, who was very respected and influential. When one of his servants became very sick and close to death, he was so concerned. He heard that Jesus was in a nearby city. Since he was a Gentile, he found some of his Jewish friends and asked them to go to Jesus and see if He would come and pray for his servant. These Jewish leaders went and pleaded with Jesus to come. Jesus agreed and set out toward the man's house. But before they arrived, this centurion sent another message. He said, "Jesus, don't trouble Yourself coming to my home. I'm a man of authority. When I say go, people go; when I say come, they come. Just speak the word, and I know my servant will be healed."

When Jesus heard this, it says, "He marveled." He was so amazed. He turned to the crowd and said, "I have not found this great a faith in all of Israel." Notice what God calls great faith. It's when you believe that He will do something out of the ordinary, when you take the limits off. No one had ever told Jesus to just speak the word. All they had seen was Jesus laying hands on people and healing them. This Roman officer was saying, "I believe You have so much power, so much favor, that You don't even have to come into my house. Just say it, and it will happen." What's significant is this centurion wasn't even a follower of Christ, but Jesus said he had more faith than the believers who traveled with Him. Having great faith is not about being a religious scholar, about how many scriptures you can quote, or about how long you pray. It's about believing that our God is all-powerful, that He can make ways where you don't see a way, that He can defeat your giants, that He can open doors you can't open.

> Having great faith is not about being a religious scholar, about how many scriptures you can quote, or about how long you pray.

There is only one other time in the Scripture when God marveled. In Mark 6, Jesus was in His hometown of Nazareth, teaching in the synagogue. They had heard about His miracles and were astonished by His wisdom. Word had spread about how Jesus was doing so much good, but they didn't believe. They thought they knew who He was. Jesus grew up there. They didn't think there was anything special about Him. Because of their unbelief, He couldn't do any mighty miracles there except to heal a few people. Here He had unlimited power, had gone to different cities and done amazing things. You would think the people in His home city would believe more than anywhere else, but it was just the opposite. It says, "Jesus marveled at their unbelief." One time, He marveled at the centurion's faith; the other time, He marveled at people's unbelief. When God looks at you, what does He marvel at? "Joel, this opposition is so strong. I

> When God looks at you, what does He marvel at?

don't see how I can get ahead. These people have done me wrong." No, zip that up. Let's be people who cause God to marvel over our faith and not over our doubt. Let's be people who believe big, pray big, people who take the limits off Him.

I love how the centurion, who didn't even worship Jehovah, who wasn't even a believer, knew how awesome our God is. He had this understanding that this Man carried power, favor, healing, and authority that was unmatched. Jesus didn't say to him, "Who do you think you are? You don't even follow Me. You have a lot of nerve, asking Me for something that I've never done." No, Jesus said, in effect, "Your faith is at another level. I've seen weak faith, little faith, and average faith, but I've never seen faith like yours. You have great faith." God is not faulting you for believing big, for asking for your dreams, for what seems impossible. That's what God calls great faith. Like this centurion, you're showing God that you believe how powerful He is. But the enemy would love for you to live with a comfortable faith, a faith in a box, a faith for what you've seen in the past. But to reach your destiny, you have to break out of that box.

> **Is there anything you're believing for that will cause God to marvel?**

Is there anything you're believing for that will cause God to marvel? Is there anything you're dreaming about that's out of your reach, that you can't accomplish, that's too big, too much, too hard? It's time to awaken your faith. Dare to believe bigger, dare to pray bolder, dare to do something that causes God to be amazed. It's time to say, "Lord, thank You that this year will be a bountiful year. Thank You that doors are opening that I couldn't open, that my talent is coming out in new ways, that I'll set a new standard for my family." Whatever level your faith is at, it's time to step it up. Believe bigger. God is doing a new thing, but it's not going to happen with a comfortable faith, a lazy faith, or a limited faith. God is looking for great faith.

Tap into Your Great Faith

In Mark 5, there was a lady who had a bleeding disorder for twelve years. She went to the best doctors, took the best treatment, but she continued to get worse. She could have accepted it and thought, *It's not meant to be. I tried my best.* But one day she heard that Jesus was passing through her town. Something rose up inside, saying, "This is your time. This is your moment. This sickness is not your destiny." Maybe she had heard how Jesus had healed a man with a withered hand, or how He'd caused a paralyzed man to walk, or how He freed the man who was living in the tombs. Something happened inside to awaken her great faith. She'd had average faith. Despite the bleeding disorder, she had been making it okay, enduring the illness, but she could sense that this was a new day.

She left her house that day determined to get to Jesus. But the streets were so crowded that she had to push through people. She had to push through the doubt. *It's not going to happen.* She had to push through her past. *You've tried everything, and it didn't work out.* She had to push through the fear. *What if He gets upset?* Despite all the opposition, she kept making her way to Jesus. "Excuse me, I need to get through. Pardon me. I don't mean to be rude, but move out of my way. I'm on a mission." She was weak because her blood count was low. Thoughts were telling her, *Why even try? Why should He care?* But she kept saying to herself, "When I get to Jesus, I will be healed." She could have stayed at home, feeling discouraged and thinking, *I'll never get better.* She could have stayed stuck with a comfortable faith, a lazy faith, but she did what I'm asking you to do. She tapped into her great faith. Yes, to believe bigger, it's going to cost you something. It's easy to stay comfortable. It's easy to live average, but you can't become who you were created to be with average faith. God is looking for great faith. He's looking for people who will cause Him

> It's easy to live average, but you can't become who you were created to be with average faith.

to marvel and say, "Wow! Look at what they believe I can do. They believe they can get well despite the diagnosis. They believe they can have a blessed year despite a bad economy. They believe that I'll give them a Compaq Center, that they can start their own business, that their family will be restored." Great faith gets God's attention.

This lady finally made it through the crowded streets to Jesus. Just in the nick of time, she reached out and touched the hem of His robe. Instantly, she was healed. Jesus stopped and asked His disciples, "Who just touched me?" They said, "What do You mean? Everybody's touching You in this crowd." "No," He said, "someone touched Me with so much faith that it drew the miracle-working power right out of Me." About that moment, His eyes met this woman's eyes. He didn't say, "Lady, why did you do that? Why didn't you wait your turn? It takes a lot of nerve for you to touch Me without My permission." No, He was amazed. He said, "Daughter, your faith has made you whole." He was saying, "It wasn't My faith. I didn't even see you. But you had such great faith, you believed in who I am in such a great way that you caused this miracle to happen." There were a lot of people bumping into Jesus that day, but she was the only one who touched Him. Many others needed healing, breakthroughs, and favor. The mistake they made is they didn't awaken their great faith. Are there blessings you're missing because you're living with a comfortable faith, not stretching? Is there favor, promotion, and new relationships that you're not seeing because you have a lazy faith, small faith, weak faith?

> Are there blessings you're missing because you're living with a comfortable faith, not stretching?

God has put something in you, and He's just waiting for you to wake it up. It's called great faith. It's faith that causes Him to marvel. You haven't seen, heard, or imagined what God has in store for you. In the times we're living in, you are needed more than ever. The prophet Joel said, "Wake up the mighty men, wake up the mighty women." God is counting on you to make a difference, to be a blessing, to shine brightly, to set new standards. It's going to take people who are bold, who will stretch, who will get out of their comfort zones.

What God Wants to Do for You

When Jesus was on the Earth, He did so many amazing things. Yet He says, "Greater works than these shall you do." Greater works are going to require great faith. If you do your part and have great faith, God will do His part and show out in your life.

> Greater works are going to require great faith.

A friend of mine is a medical doctor. He was driving home from work when he came upon an accident on the freeway that had happened just minutes earlier. He saw that a young man had been covered with a sheet. My friend told the paramedics that he was a doctor and asked if there was anything he could do. They explained they had done CPR and tried everything on the young man, but there was no response. My friend, at that time, wasn't necessarily a strong believer. But he remembered the scripture that says you can lay hands on the sick and they will recover. Medically speaking, he couldn't do anything, but he gently placed his hands on the young man's chest. Under his breath, he whispered, "God, I'm asking You to let life come back into this body." He stayed there a minute or two, and nothing happened. He turned around and was headed back to his car when suddenly there was a huge commotion. The young man started breathing again and woke up. Everyone was in awe. They asked the doctor, "What did you do to him?" He said, "All I did was pray."

That's one of those greater works. That's what God wants to do for you. He wants to use you in amazing ways, to bring dreams to pass that leave you in awe, to take you places that you never thought possible. How does this happen? Through great faith. It's inside you right now. Have you awakened it? Or are you just living with a comfortable faith, an average faith, not believing, not stretching, not dreaming? Get out of that box. Take the limits off God. There should be something you're believing for that causes God to marvel. There should be something that's over your head, out of your range. That's what gets God's attention. If you do this, if you wake up your great faith, I believe and declare that you're going to see new levels of favor, blessing, and abundance. Dead bones are about to come back to life. You're about to see the greatness of our God show out in your life in unprecedented ways.

> He wants to use you in amazing ways, to bring dreams to pass that leave you in awe, to take you places that you never thought possible.

CHAPTER FIVE

Seeing Beyond the Logical

It's dangerous to put your human limitations on the
God who spoke worlds into existence and let your
reasoning talk you out of what He put in your heart.

On the way to your destiny, you will face dreams that you can't accomplish on your own, obstacles that are too big for you, people who come against you who are more powerful than you. When you look at the situation in the natural, when you reason it out, there's no way. Your income just isn't keeping up with inflation. Your elderly parent needs more and more of your care. The broken relationship in your family has gone on and on. All of your logic says, "Just accept it. It's not meant to be." This is what faith is all about. God will put you in situations on purpose where there is no solution in the natural. That's a test. Are you going to get discouraged and give up on your dreams, or are you going to walk by faith and not by sight?

In Matthew 16, Jesus said to Peter, "You are a dangerous trap to Me. You are thinking merely from a human point of view, and not from God's." It's significant that He used such a strong word. He said, "Peter, it's dangerous to

> The reason He said "dangerous" is that you can miss your destiny if you only look at things from a natural perspective.

look at it only from the logical." He could have said, "Peter, you need to have more faith. You need to think better, to be a little more positive." The reason He said "dangerous" is that you can miss your destiny if you only look at things from a natural perspective.

God is supernatural. When you get in agreement with Him, there is a force behind you that will make things happen that you can't make happen. You're not doing life on your own. The Most High God is breathing in your direction. Don't be limited by your logic. Logic can be a dream stealer. If you look at your situation only from a human point of view—what you can do, your resources, your connections, your experience—you're going to miss the greatness God put in you.

> **Logic can be a dream stealer.**

The Limitations of Human Reasoning

The book of Genesis tells about how God created the heavens and the Earth. On the first day, He said, "Let there be light," and light came. On the second day, He separated the waters from the sky. On the third day, He created plants and trees. On the fourth day, He made the sun and the moon. What's interesting is that there was light on the first day, but He didn't make the sun until the fourth day. How can you have light without the sun? God was showing us that He's not limited to the logical. He's supernatural. He's going to do things in your life that are unexplainable, things that don't make sense. How could my mother be alive forty-three years after being diagnosed with terminal cancer? That's not logical. That defies the odds. That's the God we serve. How could I be pastoring today? When my father passed,

> **How can you have light without the sun?**

I didn't have the training or the experience. I've never been to seminary. But God doesn't choose the way we choose. He does things that are uncommon, unusual, out of the ordinary. God being for you is more than the world being against you. You may have some big obstacles, but you have to remind yourself that we serve a big God. Sometimes He'll let the odds be against you on purpose so that when He turns it around, it will be a bigger miracle.

The promises God put in your heart, what He's whispered to you in the night, may not seem possible. It may seem too big, it's never happened for your family, and you don't have the necessary experience. All your logic says there's no way. That's okay. Jesus says, "Humanly speaking, it is impossible, but with God all things are possible." Here's the question. Are you going to let your human reasoning, what you can see, what's natural, set the limits for your life? Or are you going to see beyond the logical? Are you going to believe that the all-powerful Creator of the universe, the God who flung stars into space, the God who parted the Red Sea, the God who brings light without the sun, will make a way where you don't see a way?

> **Are you going to let your human reasoning, what you can see, what's natural, set the limits for your life?**

The Impossible Becomes Possible

This is what happened with a teenager named Mary who was living in Nazareth, engaged to a young man named Joseph. An angel appeared to her and said, "Mary, you will give birth to a son without knowing a man. You are to name Him Jesus." The Scripture says Mary was confused and disturbed, which is easy to understand. God just gave her a promise that seemed impossible. You can't have a baby without a man. That defies the laws of nature. Mary said to the angel, "How can I have a child? I'm a virgin." The angel said, "The Spirit of the Most High will come upon you and cause you to conceive." The angel didn't get upset because she didn't believe. He didn't say, "Too bad, Mary, but you just blew it. God promised it, but you didn't have enough faith." He simply helped her have a new perspective. He was saying, in effect, "Mary, you're looking at it in the natural; and you're right, it is impossible. In your own ability, it won't happen. But the Spirit of God will make it happen." I believe that God sent me, like this angel, to help you have the right perspective. There is a force that you can't see, a power that will cause the impossible to become possible.

Mary was at a critical point. What she did next would determine whether she would have the baby. She could have said to the angel, "I don't think so. You need to go back to school and take biology. You can't have a baby without a man." But Mary did what we all have to do. She looked beyond the logical. She didn't let her human reasoning talk her out of it. She said to the angel, "Let it be to me according to your word." She was saying, "God, I don't see how. It seems impossible, but I'm in agreement with You. Let it happen."

As with Mary, God is going to put promises in your heart that don't

> The Spirit of the living God will make the promise happen. It's going to be supernatural, something you can't explain, something you can't take credit for.

make sense. There's no way you can get well, no way you can get your business off the ground, no way you can have a baby. Perhaps you've gone through all the fertility treatments. You've been told no again and again. You're right where Mary was. Are you going to keep seeing it only from a human point of view, or are you going to get in agreement with God and believe what the angel said?

How can this happen? It's not going to be your own strength, your own intellect, or your own hard work. The Spirit of the living God will make the promise happen. It's going to be supernatural, something you can't explain, something you can't take credit for. Everyone will know that it's the hand of God.

I talked with a man who had cancer on his vocal cords and was in Houston for surgery. He stopped by the church and asked us to pray for him. The doctors were going to remove most of his vocal cords. He was told that he would be able to make sounds, but he wouldn't be able to talk. From a human perspective, it didn't look good. The odds were against him. I told him what I'm telling you: God has the final say. He controls the universe. When you believe, all things are possible. A few weeks later, he was back at church. He came up to me, speaking as clearly as the first time we met. I said, "What happened? You didn't have the surgery, did you?" He smiled real big and said, "Yes, I had the surgery, but I can still speak like before." Ninety percent of his vocal cords were removed and he can still talk normally. The doctors can't explain it. The surgeon said that in all his years of practice, he's never seen or heard of this. That's God bringing light without a sun, bringing a baby without a man.

"Is There Anything Too Hard?"

In John 8, Jesus said to the Pharisees, "You judge me with all your human limitations." Don't put your human limitations on the God who spoke worlds into existence. God is not limited by the laws of medicine, the laws of economics, the laws of nature, the laws of science. When He is ready

> **Don't put your human limitations on the God who spoke worlds into existence.**

to bless you, He doesn't check with your boss or look at your 401(k). He doesn't google the stock market report. He doesn't consider the friends you have or what family you come from. He's not moved by the natural. He's supernatural.

I mentioned previously that after the Israelites' exodus from Egypt, the people complained to Moses that they were tired of eating the manna every day. Moses went to God and said, "These people want meat. Where am I to get meat for all these people in the desert?" God said, "Moses, that's no problem for me. I'll give them meat for a whole month." Moses said, "God, that's impossible. Do you see where we are? If we butchered all of our flocks and herds, we wouldn't have enough meat for even one meal for two million people." There were no grocery stores out there, no Uber Eats, no Domino's delivery. From a logical perspective, Moses was right. But God defies logic. He's not limited by what limits us. One touch of His favor and the impossible becomes possible. God shifted the winds and millions of quail flew into their camp. They were three or four feet off the ground, and the people grabbed all they wanted. For a month, they had quail dinners out in the middle of the desert.

What's significant is that quail don't normally fly that far away from water. You'd never find a quail in the middle of that desert unless it was migrating, but God controls the universe. If you take the limits off Him, He'll cause opportunity to find you. Good breaks will chase you down. The right people will come knocking at your door. Don't do like Moses and tell God all the reasons you can't be blessed, you can't get well, you can't accomplish your dream. You're studying the facts, the circumstances, what people say, what normally happens. The problem is that you're being limited by your logic. You're seeing it only from a human point of view. God says that's dangerous. You can miss your quail,

> You're seeing it only from a human point of view. God says that's dangerous.

miss your promotion, miss your breakthrough. Have a new perspective. *God, I'm in the desert. It seems impossible to me, but I know that You can do the impossible. You make rivers in the desert. You turn shepherds into kings. You bring babies out of barren wombs. You open doors that are deadbolted. The Scripture says, "Is there anything too hard for the Lord?"*

Power to Defy Logic

The other day I was riding my bike down a long path toward downtown Houston. There was a young man on a skateboard a couple hundred yards in front of me. I rode about five minutes and noticed that I wasn't gaining on him. I thought, *That's strange. I'm on a large bike with big wheels and pedaling fast. He's on that little skateboard with little three-inch wheels, yet he's outpacing me.* At one point, we were both going up a large hill and he was just scooting along, no problem. I was huffing and puffing, trying to get up the hill. He was doing it with such ease. It didn't make sense to me. He turned and went a different way, but about thirty minutes later I saw him sitting on a park bench. He had his skateboard turned over on its side. What I didn't realize is that his skateboard had a motor on it. He had the remote control in his hand. The reason he was going faster and farther with less effort is he had an advantage. He had something I couldn't see.

In the same way, as a child of the Most High God, you have an advantage. There is a force breathing in your direction that's going to cause you to defy the odds. You're going to go further, faster, with less struggle. People are going to look at you and not understand

> There is a force breathing in your direction that's going to cause you to defy the odds.

it. People will think, *How could you get out of that neighborhood? I saw how you were raised.* They're looking at it from a human point of view. What they can't see is that you have a motor, an anointing, a favor, a blessing on your life. "How could you lead your company in sales? You don't have the experience." Logically speaking, they're correct, but what God is doing in your life is going to defy logic. "How could you beat that sickness? The medical report said no way." Yes, but there's another report you can't see. Jehovah Rapha, "the Lord our healer," is breathing on your life.

> **Don't judge your future by your human limitations.**

Don't judge your future by your human limitations. What God is about to do in your life is going to amaze you—the doors He's about to open, the influence He's going to give you, the resources, the ideas, the creativity, the divine connections.

The enemy would love to keep you stuck with a limited mindset that's focused only on the logical. My prayer is: "God, open our eyes. Help us to see what You see, not just a logical point of view, but a heavenly perspective. Help us to realize that You are all-powerful, that You are in control, that You are for us."

Faith Is of the Heart

In Acts 27, the apostle Paul had been on a boat headed to Rome for fourteen days when it was shipwrecked. Everyone on the ship swam to the shore on the small island of Malta. Paul went over to pick up some sticks to make a fire, and a poisonous snake bit his wrist, latched on and wouldn't let go. The teeth were penetrating the skin, the venom going in. The natives on the island knew exactly what was going to happen. They had seen it time and time again. When someone was bitten, the

Scripture says they would swell up, get sick, and die. The natives waited and waited and waited. The problem was that nobody told Paul he was supposed to die. Sometimes what you don't know is good for you. If you get a negative report and overanalyze it, reason it out, study it all day, that's going to take your faith. That's why the Scripture says, "Lean not to your own understanding." Take this in the right sense, but sometimes you have to turn off your mind. Faith is not of the mind; faith is of the

> **We should use common sense to make good decisions, but don't let your logic talk you out of what God put in your heart.**

heart. Yes, we should use common sense to make good decisions, but don't let your logic talk you out of what God put in your heart.

God had told Paul that he was going to stand before Caesar. Paul simply shook the snake off and went about his business. It never affected him. The people on the island were so amazed that they thought he was a god. But if Paul had made the mistake of seeing it only from a logical, human point of view, knowing that he had just been bitten by a poisonous snake, he would have been afraid. Maybe the venom would have harmed him, maybe he would have died. When things come against you, it's easy to look at it only in the natural. "Look at this delay. I never dreamed we'd have this setback. What are we going to do?" But you have to remind yourself that God is still on the throne. Nothing can snatch you out of His hands. He wouldn't allow it if He didn't already have a solution.

Our family knew a man named Casey when I was growing up. He owned a company that moved houses. One day they had traveled several hours down country roads moving a house, having to raise the power lines and move signage to clear the way. They finally made it to their destination when Casey realized they had forgotten the main chain that was needed to unload the house. It was several hours back to the city, late in the day, and he didn't want to leave the house on the side of the road. He told his men that he was going to pray and ask God to give him a chain. They kind of snickered and one of them said sarcastically, "What are you going to do? Pray that God rains down a chain from Heaven?" Then they all laughed and made fun of it. Casey said, "God, I know there's nothing too hard for You. I don't see how this can happen in the natural, nothing in my logic says this makes sense, but I know that You're supernatural. You have ways that I've never thought of, so I'm asking You to give me a chain." All his

> **When you're not limited by your logic, you'll pray bold prayers.**

men were rolling their eyes and shaking their heads. But Jesus said, "Don't judge Me with your human limitations. Don't put Me in the same category of what you can do. I am all-powerful." When you're not limited by your logic, you'll pray bold prayers. You'll shake off a snake like Paul did, a bad break or a disappointment, and go about your business. You'll believe for your dreams, for what looks unlikely.

Casey and his men were standing on the side of the road out in the middle of nowhere, trying to figure out what they were going to do. There was a sharp curve in the road right in front of them. About that time an old beat-up pickup truck with its tailgate open came barreling down the road going way too fast. When it took the curve, a chain slung out of the back of the bed, slid across the road, and curled up at Casey's feet. He picked it up and said, "Here's my chain, boys. Let's go to work." Is there anything too hard for the Lord?

The Laughter of Amazement

Are you basing your prayers on your ability, your connections, your finances? If you only see things from a natural, logical point of view, you're going to miss the fullness of what God has in store. It's dangerous to limit Him to only what you think can happen. Take the limits off. Pray some bold prayers. Dream some big dreams. If you can accomplish your dream in your own ability, with your connections, and your finances, your dream is too small. God has things in your future that you haven't seen, levels that you haven't imagined. Don't limit Him to the logical. Choose to believe even when your mind says, "That's too far out. You'll never get well, never start your business, never see your family restored." When all the odds are against you, you're in a perfect position for God to show out in your life, to do something that you've never seen.

> When all the odds are against you, you're in a perfect position for God to show out in your life, to do something that you've never seen.

God told Abraham and Sarah that they were going to have a baby when they were both way too old. When Sarah heard it, the Scripture says that she laughed and said, "How could a worn-out woman like me have a baby?" She thought, *That's so far out, it's funny. It's comical. Imagine me having a child.* Sarah did what many of us do. She looked at it only in the natural. In her human reasoning, she was right. You can't have a baby at ninety years old. But when God puts a promise in your heart, when He whispers something to you in your spirit, it may seem so far out, so unlikely, that you could easily dismiss it. Try a different approach. Do as Mary did and say, "God, let it happen. I'm in agreement with You. I don't see how, but I'm not going to limit You to my human point of view." When Sarah was ninety years old, against all odds, she gave birth to a son. The Scripture says that she laughed again and said, "God has brought me laughter, and all who hear about this will laugh with me." She even named her son Isaac, which means "laughter."

The first time she laughed in unbelief, thinking, *There's no way.*

The second time she laughed in amazement, thinking, *Look what the Lord has done.* In the past, you may have laughed in unbelief, thinking that what God promised you could never come to pass. You discounted it and said, "It's too late. It's too big. It's impossible." The good news is that didn't stop the promise. I believe that your second laugh is coming. God is about to do something so awesome, so big, that you're going to laugh in amazement. The second laugh is going to surprise you. It's going to be something out of the ordinary, something you can't explain, something that catapults you to a new level. Get ready. God is about to defy the odds. He's about to show out in your life. You haven't seen, heard, or imagined what He's about to do. Like Sarah, you're going to stand in awe at the greatness of our God. You wouldn't be reading this if that second laugh wasn't on the way.

> The second laugh is going to surprise you. It's going to be something out of the ordinary, something you can't explain, something that catapults you to a new level.

Now do your part. Don't see things only from a human point of view. Don't let your logic limit what God wants to do. I'm not saying to deny the facts, to act as though they don't exist. I'm saying to see beyond the logical. Get a heavenly perspective. The Most High God is on your side. He hasn't forgotten what He promised you. If you do this, I believe and declare that you're going to see supernatural provision, unexpected favor, and new doors are about to open. The right people, the right breaks, and the solutions are already on the way.

CHAPTER SIX

Receive When You Believe

If you're praying and then worrying, asking God for the same thing over and over, the problem is that you're really not receiving what you're asking for.

We all have things we're believing for. One day we're going to get well, one day we're going to break the addiction, one day we're going to meet the right person. We've prayed; we're standing in faith waiting for it to happen. But Jesus gives us an important principle in Mark 11. He says, "Whatever you ask for in prayer, believe that you have received it, and it will be yours." He didn't say believe that it's going to happen or believe that you're going to see things turn around. He said to believe that you receive when you pray. Believe that it happened right then—not in a week, not in a month. Believe that right when you prayed, things changed in your favor. God has set the miracle into motion. If you're facing an illness, you have to say, "God, I'm asking You to heal my body. And, Lord, I receive my healing right now." When you not only pray but you take it a step further and receive your healing, in the unseen realm things begin to happen. But if the healing, the freedom, the promotion, or the breakthroughs are

> What God is going to bring to pass is not what you asked for but what you believe you receive when you pray.

always in your future, you haven't received it into your spirit. What God is going to bring to pass is not what you asked for but what you believe you receive when you pray.

Are you receiving when you're believing? This means not just saying, "God, I'm asking You to free me from this addiction. Help me to break this bad habit." That's good, but that is not enough. Follow it up with, "Lord, I receive Your freedom. Thank You that I am free." It's not, "I'm going to be free. I'm hoping one day to break the addiction. I'm really struggling in this area." No, it's already happened. When you prayed, you not only believed but you received it. Now change your report from "I'm hoping for it" to "It's already done." It's just a matter of time before what happened in the unseen realm shows up in the natural realm. You have to be healed in your spirit before you'll be healed in your body. You have to be prosperous in your spirit before you'll be prosperous in the natural. If you believe that it's going to happen sometime in the future, there's no promise that it's going to happen. You have to receive it when you believe. When you pray, even though nothing seems to have changed, even though every circumstance looks the same, your faith says, "It happened. Things changed in my favor."

Enter into Rest

This is what my mother did when she was diagnosed with terminal liver cancer in 1981. There was no medical treatment they could give her. When my father brought her home from the hospital, they were devastated. They lay down on the bedroom floor, prayed, and asked God to heal her. My mother believed that she received her healing that day—not that she was going to be healed, but that it had already happened. She wrote it down: *December 11, 1981. When we prayed, healing came into my body.* She didn't look any different, and she didn't feel any different, but she didn't go by what she saw or felt. We have to walk by faith and not by sight. From that time on, I never heard her pray, "God, please heal me. Please let me live. Please turn this around." If you receive it when you pray, then instead of begging God, you'll thank Him. "Lord, thank You that I am healed. Thank You that with long life You will satisfy me." If you're asking God for the same thing over and over, the problem is that you're not receiving what you're asking for. Try a different approach and believe that it happened.

For months, my mother didn't look any better. She was frail, and her skin was yellow. But I would hear her going through the house, saying, "Father, thank You that when we prayed on December 11, healing came into my body. Lord, I believe the tide of the battle turned in my health on that day." Her mind was made up. She was no longer trying to get healed; she was already healed. She was just waiting for the manifestation to show up. That's different than hoping something will happen. When you pray according to God's Word, and you receive what you're believing for, there's a certainty. It's already happened. You don't have to live worried, trying to convince God to do something. You can rest, knowing that it's already done. At the right time, God will bring it from the unseen to the seen. This is a much better way to live. This takes all the pressure off. If you're praying and then worrying, asking God again and again, stressed out, you really didn't receive it. The Scripture says, "Those who have believed enter into rest." When you've received it by faith, you don't live uptight. You know it's in God's hands.

> When you pray according to God's Word, and you receive what you're believing for, there's a certainty. It's already happened.

My mother kept thanking God for her healing. Over time, what she received in her spirit became a reality in the natural. She got better and better. Over forty years later, she's still healthy and strong. I believe one key is that she received her healing when she prayed. She believed she was healed when there was no sign of it. Jesus didn't say, "Believe you receive when you see it, when your health turns around, when the breakthrough comes." He said, in effect, "Believe you receive when you pray, when nothing looks any different, when it seems as though the sickness is winning, when your finances aren't changing." If it happened instantly, it wouldn't take any faith. This is where you show God what you're made of.

The test is when we don't see anything changing. Thoughts whisper, *Nothing happened. You didn't get healed. You're just the same. Something would have improved by now. You prayed, but you'll never meet the right person. You asked, but your business is not going to make it.* Don't believe those lies. The enemy would love to talk you out of what God put in your spirit. You received it by faith, now you have to walk by faith. Just because you don't see anything happening doesn't mean God is not working. In the unseen realm, what you received in your spirit became a reality. It's just a matter of time before it shows up.

It's Just a Matter of Time

In Matthew 21, when Jesus and His disciples were leaving the city of Bethany, He saw a fig tree in the distance. He was hungry, so He walked over to it, but it didn't have any figs on it. He said to the tree, "May no person ever eat your fruit again." But when He said it, nothing on the outside of the tree looked any different. It was just as healthy looking and green as ever. I can hear the disciples whispering, "What happened? It didn't work this time." They had seen Him speak to a blind man and his eyes were healed. They heard Him speak to a storm and calm the waters, but when He spoke to this tree, nothing changed. There was no evidence that what He said had happened. The disciples went on their way, puzzled and wondering what went wrong. The next morning, however, as they were passing by the tree, the disciples saw that it was withered. Peter was so amazed that he said, "Look, Jesus! The tree you cursed is dying." They thought nothing happened after Jesus spoke, nothing looked any different, but in the unseen realm things changed.

Jesus then told them this principle: "When you pray, believe that you receive it, and you will have it." He was showing us through the fig tree that you may not see anything changing. All the evidence may look the same. Your health is the same. Your finances haven't improved. Your children haven't gotten back on course. You could think, *God, I received my healing. I received what You promised, but I don't feel any different. I'm still struggling in my career. I'm still waiting for the right person. Maybe I'm not healed. Maybe I'm not prosperous. Maybe I won't meet the right person.* No, don't be fooled by the outside. God is working behind the scenes. In the realm that you can't see,

> **Don't be fooled by the outside. God is working behind the scenes. In the realm that you can't see, things have shifted.**

things have shifted. The moment you received what you believed for, things started lining up in your favor and heading your way—good breaks, the right people, healing, abundance.

The Scripture says, "The roots of the fig tree began to wither." Something underground, something unseen, began to take place. Right now, there are things in the unseen realm changing in your favor. Chains that have held you back are being broken. Bad habits that have hindered your children are being loosed. Strongholds are coming down. New doors are about to open. Dreams you've been believing for are about to show up. Don't get discouraged by what's not happening. You can't see into this unseen realm. This is where faith kicks in. "God, I don't see any evidence, nothing looks like it's improving, but I know what I received in my spirit is about to show up in the natural."

Jesus started off this passage by saying, "Have faith in God." It's not faith in your circumstances. It's not faith in what you can do. It's not faith in your boss, your banker, your parents, your doctor, or your pastor. That's all good. But they don't control the universe. They didn't speak worlds into existence. They didn't part the Red Sea or raise Lazarus from the dead. Our God is all-powerful. Nothing can stand against Him. When He speaks, angels go to work, forces of darkness are broken, good breaks come chasing you down. What you've received in your spirit may look impossible, and the odds are against you, but it's nothing for our God. One touch of His favor will catapult you ahead, free you from the addiction, heal you from the illness, cause you to come out of lack into abundance, out of struggle into overflow, out of loneliness into great relationships.

You may be looking at a fig tree today and saying, "Joel, I received my healing, but nothing happened. I believe I'm blessed, I'm prosperous, and I'm free, but there's no sign of it." Stay in faith; your time is coming. God is faithful. He sees you doing the right thing. He sees you believing when you're not seeing, praising when you could be complaining, thanking Him when it's not improving. It's just a matter of time before you see the breakthrough, the promotion, the healing, the victory. Don't get talked out of it. Don't let what's not happening convince you that God is not working in the unseen realm. Everything starts in the unseen, and it is through our faith that we bring it into the seen.

> Everything starts in the unseen, and it is through our faith that we bring it into the seen.

You Don't Have to Keep Asking

When my father passed in 1999, I knew I was supposed to step up and pastor the church even though I had never ministered. When I first started, I was so nervous, so intimidated, so insecure. Every thought told me I couldn't get up in front of people. I prayed and asked God to help me, asked for confidence, asked for strength, but I didn't understand this principle that you have to receive it when you ask. I was waiting to feel confident, to feel anointed. The problem was that the feeling never came. I kept asking God again and again. One day, I realized what I'm telling you. I had to receive it by faith. Instead of saying, "God, help me to be confident. Help me to be strong. I'm asking for your anointing," I started believing and saying, "I am anointed. I am confident. I am strong. I am well able." When I was saying that, I felt just the opposite. It was like the fig tree. "God, You said it, You promised it, but I don't see any evidence." I just kept saying it, kept believing it, kept declaring it, and before long it became a reality. I pulled it out of the unseen into the seen.

Once you ask God for something, you don't have to keep asking. The key is to receive it, believe that it happened, and then instead of asking over and over, start thanking Him. I quit asking God for His anointing and started saying, "Father, thank You that I am anointed." I don't ask God to bless me every day because I've received the blessing. I say, "Father, thank You that I am blessed. Thank You that I am prosperous. Thank You that I am healthy." If you continue to ask for the same thing over and over, I know you're sincere, but that's not showing God that you trust Him.

If our daughter, Alexandra, asked me for something and I said, "Yes, I'll do it," but then she came back later with the same request and asked me again and again and again, that would make me feel bad as her father. I would think, *Don't you trust me? I said I would do it. You don't have to keep asking me.* It's the same way with our Heavenly Father. When you ask, that's fine. But Jesus said to not stop there, but believe that you received what you asked for. Believe that your Father loves you so much, that He's so good, so kind, that He granted your request, that He said yes to what you're asking for. Yes to the healing, yes to the favor, yes to the wisdom, yes to the breakthrough. The apostle John says, "This is the confidence we have in God, if we ask anything according to His will, He hears us. And we know that He will give us whatever we ask." If you're asking according to God's will, you can be confident. Yes is the answer. You don't have to beg, you don't have to wonder, just receive His yes by faith.

> Believe that your Father loves you so much, that He's so good, so kind, that He granted your request, that He said yes to what you're asking for.

You can find God's will in His Word. He says that He wishes above all things that you prosper and be in good health. He says that He's crowned you with favor, that you will lend and not borrow, that your children are mighty in the land. He says that you will leave your mark, that you are a mighty hero. His will is found in His Word. It's full of His promises. After you pray, "Father, I'm asking that my children will be mighty in the land," then receive it by faith, believe that it happened. From then on just say, "Lord, thank You that my children are mighty in the land," not, "Please, God, won't You do something with them?" Receive what you're believing for. "Father, You said whatever I touch will prosper and succeed. I'm asking for Your blessing on my business. Let my gifts come out to the full and cause me to shine brightly." Now don't keep praying that same prayer every day. Take the next step. "Father, I receive what You promised. Thank You that I am blessed, that I am prosperous, that I'm a difference maker, that I will leave my family better than they were before."

The way you pull it out of the unseen into the seen is by faith. It's by receiving what you're asking for.

Be Confident in Shifts in the Unseen

Here's another key to receiving answers to prayer: It doesn't do any good to pray for something and then go out and talk about how it's probably not going to happen. Don't cancel out your prayer with negative talk. "We prayed for our finances, Joel, but I don't know. Have you seen the news? This economy is rough." You just nullified your prayer. You can't pray for victory and talk defeat. When you believe that you received what you asked for, that it already happened, it's a different mindset. It's not, "I hope it's going to work out." There's a knowing. Your attitude is: *It's already done. Things have shifted in my favor.* This is the confidence we can have in our God. He's called El Shaddai, the God of more than enough. He's called Jehovah Jireh, the Lord our provider. He's called Jehovah Rapha, the Lord our healer. He's called the Great I AM, the all-sufficient One. When we ask in faith, when we receive it into our spirit, we can be confident that in the unseen realm something shifts. Favor is set in motion. Angels are dispatched. Forces of darkness are broken. It's not, "I wonder *if* it's going to happen." No, "It's *when* it's going to happen. I am confident in the God we serve, that He is faithful, that what He started, He will finish." It may look like the fig tree right now, like nothing has changed, but you know a secret. In the unseen realm, things have changed. It's just a matter of time before you receive what you saw in your spirit.

A while back a mother came for prayer for her teenage daughter

> **Don't cancel out your prayer with negative talk.**

during a service. She told how her daughter was off course, running with the wrong crowd, and wasn't being respectful. She was so concerned. We prayed that this young lady would turn around and start making good decisions. The next week this mother came down with the same request, telling how it wasn't getting any better, and this time she went on and on. My heart went out to her. We prayed again. The following week, she was back again with the same request. I told her what I'm telling you. We don't have to keep praying for the same thing. We either believe that God answered the first time, that He set the miracle in motion, or we don't. At this point, it's not up to God, it's up to us. Jesus says that whatever you ask for, believe that you receive it when you pray—not when you see it manifest, not when it turns around. The test is whether you receive what you're believing for.

> **We either believe that God answered the first time, that He set the miracle in motion, or we don't.**

We can pray all day long, but if we go out and talk defeat, if we call our friends and say, "I don't see how it's going to happen," we're canceling out the prayer. The problem is that you didn't receive when you believed. If you had received it, you would have a different mindset. You're confident that it's already done. You're not walking by sight; you're walking by faith. You're not moved by what you don't see. You know things are happening in the unseen realm. When doubt comes, discouraging thoughts whisper, *Hey, nothing happened. Look at the fig tree. It's still the same.* Instead of getting discouraged and speaking defeat, switch over into praise. "Father, thank You that I am healed. Thank You that my son is mighty in the land. Thank You that my business is blessed." We're not hoping so, not thinking it's going to be some day in the future. "Lord, thank You that it's already done."

Come Expecting an Answer

The Scripture says in the book of James, "If you need wisdom, you can ask God and He will gladly tell you. But when you ask, be sure you really expect Him to answer. For a doubtful mind is as unsettled as a wave of the sea. People like that should not expect to receive anything from God." This is talking about receiving wisdom, but the principle is true: When you ask God, be sure you really expect Him to answer. Sometimes we go to God hoping, wishing, *Maybe I'll get lucky and something will happen.* How about going to God with confidence, knowing that when you ask in faith, He will answer you? I love how it says that God will gladly give you wisdom. He's not up in the heavens upset as though you're bothering Him and saying, "What do you need again? I'm tired of dealing with you." God loves for you to come to Him. He's longing

> How about going to God with confidence, knowing that when you ask in faith, He will answer you?

to be good to you. But if you're going to see things happen, there are some requirements. First, come to Him expecting an answer, expecting Him to be good to you. And second, when you ask, believe that you receive it. By faith, believe that it happened.

James says that when you're double-minded, you can't expect to receive anything from God. He asks, "How long will you waver between two opinions?" You have to make up your mind. Are you going to believe what God promised you, or are you going to let doubt and negative voices convince you it's not going to happen? "What if this doesn't work out? You'll never get that contract. You'll never be successful." Do yourself a favor and tune that out. Don't let doubt keep you from your destiny. Have an unwavering mind that says, "My mind is made up. I believe that I received it when I prayed;

now my mind is set. I'm not moved by what I don't see. I'm not going to let other people talk me out of it. I'm not going to let time convince me that it's not going to happen. I'm not going to let the fig tree cause me to waver. I believe it's already done."

Doubt comes to us all. You have to guard your mind. You control the doorway to your thoughts. When those negative thoughts come, have a "No Vacancy" sign. "Sorry, no room for you here. My mind is filled with faith. I am healthy. I am blessed. I am anointed. I am victorious." Don't give any energy to the negative. When you dwell on negative thoughts and start going down the road of all the things that are not going to work out, you're giving life to those thoughts. You're allowing them to grow. Start starving your doubts and feeding your faith. As the Scripture says, you may have been wavering between two opinions, going back and forth. One day you say, "I believe it's going to happen." The next day you say, "It's never going to work out." You've been unsettled. That's okay. Today can be a new day. You can set your mind. You can make the decision: "When I pray, I'm not just going to believe that it will happen, I'm going to believe that it did happen. I'm going to receive it when I believe."

> You control the doorway to your thoughts. When those negative thoughts come, have a "No Vacancy" sign.

You may have been doing this already. Like my mother, you've been standing in faith when nothing is improving, believing when you're not seeing, thanking God when there's no sign of it. Thoughts tell you that God has forgotten about you, and it's never going to change. No, you need to get ready. Your time is coming. I believe and declare that what's in the unseen realm is about to become a reality in your life. You're about to rise higher, overcome obstacles, accomplish dreams, and fulfill His plan for your life.

CHAPTER SEVEN

Unquestionably Free

God is going to put an end to the things that are
limiting you, holding you back, draining your joy,
burdening you down, and keeping you from walking in
the fullness of the blessing.

When we've struggled in an area for a long time, it's easy to accept that's the way it's always going to be. We did everything we could do. We prayed, we stood in faith, but nothing changed. Now we think, *I'll always have this sickness. I'll always struggle in my finances. I'll always deal with this anxiety, this depression. I'll always have this trouble at work.* We're functioning, we're making it, but it's restricting our joy, limiting our growth. Recently, a man told me that he's tried to forgive the people who did him wrong, but he can't get past it. He is still bitter and angry toward them. Now it's keeping him from moving forward. But God didn't create you to be partially free, to be almost free, to be better than you used to be. The Scripture says, "Whom the Son sets free is unquestionably free." The things that are hindering you, that are keeping you from your potential, are not permanent. The sickness is not how your story ends. Don't believe the lie that you have to live with the depression or the addiction. No, God is about to do something new in your life.

You're coming into a shift, a breakthrough. What you couldn't

> **Your destiny is too great and your time is too valuable for you to go another year living restricted, being limited.**

do on your own, God is going to step in and do for you. Your destiny is too great and your time is too valuable for you to go another year living restricted, being limited. You're about to see the God of the breakthrough, the God who suddenly shows up and puts an end to what's holding you back. He wants you to be unquestionably free. That freedom means there's nothing draining your joy, nothing hindering your potential, nothing limiting your relationships. Yes, there are seasons we have to endure and fight the good fight of faith, but there comes a time when God says, "Enough is enough. Now I'm going to step in and free you, heal you, promote you, favor you."

One Touch of His Favor

This is what happened with the Israelites. They had been in slavery for over four hundred years. Ten generations of Israelites had been mistreated and taken advantage of. It wasn't fair. Most of them were born into lack and hardship. They didn't choose it. They inherited struggles and defeat. You can imagine their mindset. *We're just slaves. We're just poor, defeated people. It's never going to change. We just have to suffer through it. We have to endure it.* They didn't see any sign of things improving. Pharaoh and his army, the ones holding them captive, had all the power, the weapons, the resources. The Israelites had nothing. But God said, "I have seen the affliction of My people, I have heard their cries, and I am coming down to deliver them." God was saying, "This is a new day. I didn't create My children to live in bondage, oppressed, and at a disadvantage. I created them to be the head and not the tail, to be above and not beneath." He didn't create you to be bound by depression, worry, lack, or mistreatment. God created you to be unquestionably free.

Pharoah and his army were one of the most powerful forces of that day. The Israelites couldn't do anything about it. The odds were against them. But God stepped in and broke the chains, parted the Red Sea, and drowned their enemies. When God says it's your time to be free, all the forces of darkness cannot stop Him. You may not see a way. The medical report says you won't get well. Your business looks like it's not going to make it. You've been to rehab, you've tried, but you couldn't break the addiction. It's been too long. The opposition is too big. You're right where the Israelites were. God is saying to you what He said to them. "I've seen your affliction. I've seen what you struggled with. I've seen the people who broke your heart. I've seen the worry, the heaviness that follows you around. I've seen the lonely nights, the tears, the suffering, and I am coming down to put an end to it." He's not just going to make it better, not just help you get through it. You're going to be unquestionably free. There's about to be a shift in your health, a shift in your finances, a shift in your children, a shift in your attitude. No more living depressed, defeated, negative, and lacking. You're going to see the hand of God do what you couldn't do on your own. It's going to be supernatural—supernatural healing, supernatural freedom, supernatural provision, supernatural favor. I met a man who was diagnosed with incurable cancer. The doctors told him he would have to come to Houston several months every year for treatment for the rest of his life. That was the only way they could control the cancer. While he was in treatment, he and his wife attended our church services. He never complained, had a good attitude, and was grateful that they had the treatment, but it was hard on him. His wife

> **When God says it's your time to be free, all the forces of darkness cannot stop Him.**

told how the chemo made him nauseous and how he didn't have any energy. She wondered how long he could keep going on like this. I told them what I'm telling you, that God sees what you're dealing with. He sees what is causing you heartache, how you're doing the right thing when it's hard, how you're being your best when nothing is improving. You can't change it. It's out of your control. That's when God in His mercy will step in and say, "Enough is enough. Let Me do what only I can do." Medicine may not be able to do it. People may not be able to help you. You've done what you can in the natural, but God is supernatural. One touch of His favor and everything will change. One touch of His healing, one touch of His provision, one touch of His goodness, and, like the Israelites, you'll be unquestionably free.

> God sees what you're dealing with. He sees what is causing you heartache, how you're doing the right thing when it's hard, how you're being your best when nothing is improving.

This man came back to Houston for his third year of treatment. They ran all the usual tests. He was prepared to do what he'd done during the previous two years—just endure, suffer through the chemo treatments. The lead doctor came in the exam room, scratching his head. He said, "Have you done anything different? Have you changed your diet, taken other medicine, found other treatment?" The man said, "All I've done is keep praying and believing that God would heal me, that He would make a way where I don't see a way." The doctor said, "It must be working because we can't find any sign of cancer in your body." The man came back a year later for his checkup. Still no cancer. They said, "There's no need to come back again. You are perfectly healthy." God has the final say. He can do what medicine cannot do.

The Chain Breaker

Is there something that's hindering you, something you can't seem to get past? Perhaps it's a negative attitude, unforgiveness, or an addiction. Maybe you just can't get ahead. You take one step forward and two steps back. It's as though a spirit of lack follows you around. That's how it's been, but there's about to be a shift, a breakthrough, a turnaround. It's not to where you're a little better, partially free, almost free, or can say, "I have no complaints." No, it's that you'll be unquestionably free, abundantly free, totally free. That means to be free from a spirit of worry, always seeing the negative. You'll be free from that hot temper, that spirit of anger that's been passed down in your family. It's going to stop with you. You'll be free from the bitterness and holding a grudge. You tried to forgive in the past but you couldn't let it go. God's about to breathe in your direction. There's going to be a strength to do what you couldn't do before. You'll be free from the guilt, living in regrets, beating yourself up, not thinking you deserve to be blessed. Those strongholds are coming down. Chains are being broken. Limitations are being lifted. What's hindered you in the past is not going to hinder you anymore.

> Is there something that's hindering you, something you can't seem to get past?

> Strongholds are coming down. Chains are being broken. Limitations are being lifted.

This is not going to happen by your own might or willpower. Maybe you've tried, and it hasn't worked out. You feel limited, as though you're at a disadvantage, at the mercy of what you're up against. That's okay. It's going to happen by the Spirit of the Most

High God. In His great mercy, He is going to release you from every bondage and free you from every restriction. You're about to step into new levels of freedom, peace, productivity, and fulfillment. Forces that were slowing you down, draining your joy, your creativity, and your potential, have been broken. Now you have to do your part and get in agreement with God. Don't go another day with an old mind-set that says, "I don't know, Joel. I've struggled with this depression, this loneliness, this compromise for a long time. I think it's always going to limit me." No, turn it around and say, "Father, thank You that I am free. This is a new day. Things have shifted in my favor. Thank You that You're releasing me into increase, into abundance, into good health, into great relationships, the fullness of my destiny."

You weren't created to struggle through life, to be restricted by negative thinking or to be constrained by a bad temper, insecurity, or lack. Those are bondages that the enemy uses to try to keep you from your destiny. The good news is, the enemy is not in control of your life. God is. He's the chain breaker. He's the burden remover. He's the yoke destroyer. He said, "I'm coming down to take off what the enemy put on you." Victory starts in our mind. It starts in our thinking. The right attitude is: *I'm supposed to be free. I'm supposed to be healthy. I'm supposed to be blessed. I'm supposed to be victorious.*

> **You weren't created to struggle through life, to be restricted by negative thinking or to be constrained by a bad temper, insecurity, or lack.**

"Do You Want to Get Well?"

In John 5, there was a man who had been crippled for thirty-eight years. Every morning, his family would carry him to the pool of

Bethesda, which was known for having healing waters. Once a year, when the angel troubled the waters, the first person into the water would be healed. There were all kinds of sick people there—the blind, crippled, and paralyzed. Every day, they would wait, eagerly watching the water, hoping that they would be the one to be healed. One afternoon, Jesus was passing by the pool and saw this man. The Scripture says, "This man had a deep seated, lingering disorder." It wasn't like he had been sick for a week or had trouble for a month. This was a problem that had lingered for thirty-eight years. You can imagine his mindset. *This is my lot in life. It's never going to change.* Out of all the people there, Jesus went over to the man and asked, "Do you want to get well?" It seemed like an odd question. It was obvious he wanted to get well. That's why he came to the pool every day. But the man answered, "How can I get well? I don't have anyone to help me get in the water. I'm crippled. Someone always gets in ahead of me."

I don't fault the man. He was only looking at it in the natural. He's thinking, *I've had this problem for most of my life. After thirty-eight years, how can I get well now?* Sometimes we see this man as doubting, as negative, but the truth is that he was faithful. He got up each morning, got dressed, had his family bring him to the pool. He sat there hoping that somehow it could happen. It wasn't that he was complacent, sitting around at home complaining, or had given up. He did all he knew how to do, but he couldn't get rid of this lingering disorder. Like this man, most people are dealing with a lingering disorder, with a problem that won't go away. Maybe it's an anxiety, a trouble in our marriage, an addiction, a sickness. We've done our best. God knows we've prayed. We've stood in faith. We said we weren't going to give in to the temptation again, but we weren't strong enough. We weren't complacent. We

> Like this man, most people are dealing with a lingering disorder, with a problem that won't go away.

still showed up at work, still came to church, still volunteered, still were good to others, and all the while we're dealing with this lingering disorder. Maybe nobody else can see it. It's the loneliness we face in the night. It's the pain we feel from the trauma of the past. It's the feelings of insecurity that won't go away.

Jesus could have looked at the man and said, "If you'd only answered, 'Yes, I want to get well,' I would have healed you. If you'd only had more faith, if you hadn't made excuses, if you hadn't just looked at it in the natural, I would have freed you from that sickness." But our God is full of mercy. He knows the weight of what you're carrying, the struggle, the sacrifice. He knows how you're doing your best to keep it all together while you're dealing with a lingering disorder—a child who's off course, a loveless marriage, an addiction that's controlling your life. God sees you at the pool. He sees you praising through the pain, smiling when you feel discouraged, carrying the load of others when you need to be carried.

> God sees you at the pool. He sees you praising through the pain, smiling when you feel discouraged, carrying the load of others when you need to be carried.

It's interesting that Jesus never addressed what the man said. He never commented on his lack of faith. He simply looked at him and said, "Rise, take up your bed, and walk." Instantly, the man was healed. He got up and walked out of there for the first time in thirty-eight years. Can you imagine when his family came to pick him up as they had done year after year? Instead, they saw him running toward them. They nearly passed out. They didn't see that coming. That's what it means to be unquestionably free. No one is going to doubt the blessing of God on your life. You're not only going to see it, but other people are going to see it.

One thing this story shows us is how nothing is permanent. It's never too late for God to turn it around. You may be dealing with a lingering disorder. In the natural, it could never work out. Thoughts tell you, *You've always struggled with your self-image. You're always going to feel inferior, not valuable.* Don't believe those lies. Your time is coming. God has not forgotten about you. He's already headed your way. You wouldn't be reading this if He weren't about to put an end to that lingering disorder. The addiction, the anxiety, the financial difficulty, the relationship issue, or the hurt from the past that's hindered you so long is about to suddenly turn around. God is going to show up and do what you never saw coming. It's something that will amaze you, something that catapults you into a new level of your destiny, to where you can do what you never thought you could do. This man never dreamed he'd be able to walk, play ball with his children, dance with his wife, or stroll down the beach. That's the mercy of our God. "Joel, this sounds good, but I don't know if I have enough faith. I don't know if I can believe for this." Neither did this man. This shows us how good our God is. Even when we don't have the faith, even when we don't believe as we should, He still steps in and frees us, heals us, favors us.

> Even when we don't have the faith, even when we don't believe as we should, He still steps in and frees us, heals us, favors us.

What Could You Become?

What could you become if you didn't have that lingering thing that holds you back, that little voice that's convinced you that you're not talented enough, you don't have what it takes, you've made too many mistakes? How far could you go if you didn't have that temper to hold you back? What would life be like if you weren't giving in to temptation or were able to forgive the people who hurt you? Or maybe it's things you were born into—the lack, depression, addictions, living with guilt and shame. The good news is, God is not going to leave you with that lingering disorder. It's lingered long enough. This is your time to be unquestionably free. It won't be where you say, "I'm doing better, making it okay. I don't have as many issues." No, get ready for total freedom. You are going to rise, take up your bed, and walk.

Jesus could have said to the crippled man, "I'm going to get you a better mat to lay on. I'm going to get you some more help, better friends, better transportation." But God's idea of freedom is not to make you more comfortable in your dysfunction. It's to free you from the dysfunction. It's to set you on a whole new path to where you look back and say, "That lingering disorder is no longer lingering. It's gone. I'm free. I'm healed. I'm confident. My marriage is healthy. My children are blessed. My career is flourishing. My mind is at peace. I'm full of joy and fulfilling my purpose."

> **God's idea of freedom is not to make you more comfortable in your dysfunction. It's to free you from the dysfunction.**

Sometimes a lingering disorder is just an underlying pressure, worries, always thinking something is wrong. We don't realize how much of our joy and creativity that takes. When I first started ministering, it was difficult, but God gave me grace and the church began to grow. Our media outreaches increased. Stations all over the country were putting on our program. My books were taking off. We got the Compaq Center. It was more than I could ever imagine. But despite

> **Sometimes a lingering disorder is just an underlying pressure, worries, always thinking something is wrong.**

all the growth, all the favor, deep down I had this feeling that something could go wrong. As we gained more influence, there was more opposition. There were people who didn't like what we were doing. Practically every week I would hear that another minister or group was talking negatively about us. I knew God was in control, and I knew He was fighting our battles, but there was still this pressure, this uneasiness, to the point where I had to fight being worried. I kept thinking, *What if it doesn't work out? What if I don't know what to speak on next week? What if the funds don't come in? What's going to happen?*

Eleven years went by. I just learned to deal with that pressure and not give in to those thoughts. But one morning in 2010, I woke up and noticed the pressure wasn't there. I didn't feel that sense of worry, that feeling that something could go wrong, at all. It was like a weight was lifted off me. I felt God say, "Joel, what I have blessed, no person can curse. I have put you in this position, and you can be assured that I will keep you in this position." I hadn't known how to get rid of that pressure, but the Most High God stepped in and said, "This lingering disorder is coming to an end." You're going to see some of these same shifts. God is going to put an end to things that are draining your joy, stealing your creativity, keeping you from walking in the fullness of the blessing. It's one thing to be blessed and successful, but it's another thing when something interferes to the point where you can't really enjoy the blessing. Maybe it's family trouble, an addiction, a worried mindset, or regrets from the past. It may be there now, but that's not how your story ends. God knows exactly what's hindering you. He's coming down to do something about it.

> God is going to put an end to things that are draining your joy, stealing your creativity, keeping you from walking in the fullness of the blessing.

Your Seventh Year

In Deuteronomy 15, God gave Moses a law for the people of Israel that said every seventh year any Hebrew slave had to be released. If you were Hebrew and you owed a person money but couldn't pay, that person could take you as a slave and make you work until you paid them back. But every seventh year, if you were a part of God's chosen people, you had an advantage. You were released. No matter how much you owed, no matter how much debt you were in, there was freedom in the seventh year. In one day, all the pain, suffering, and heartache was gone. This shows us that God never intended for His people to be permanent slaves to anything. He had Moses write this law so they wouldn't live with a lingering disorder—a slave to debt, a slave to addiction, a slave to worry.

You may be dealing with some negative things now, but I believe you're coming into your seventh year. You're going to see God break limitations, free you from what's holding you back, lift the load of what's been burdening you down. As God did for me when I suddenly felt that weight lift off me, God is about to lighten your load. You're going to see an anointing of ease. God is breathing in your direction. Things are about to shift. Where there has been a spirit of worry and insecurity, to where you can't sleep at night, there's going to be a peace, a rest, a new sense of joy. You're going from being stressed over your children to enjoying your children. You're going from worrying about a sickness to having great health. You're going from struggling with lack, not having enough, to abundance, to overflow, to where you can be a blessing to others.

> God is about to lighten your load. You're going to see an anointing of ease. God is breathing in your direction.

Get ready for a seventh year. It's not partial freedom, not a little bit better, but unquestionably free. God is doing a new thing. You're stepping into a new season. I believe and declare that every limitation that's been holding you back is being broken right now. Things are shifting. Strongholds are coming down. Favor is being released. Lingering disorders are coming to an end. You're going to step into

> **It's not partial freedom, not a little bit better, but unquestionably free.**

new levels of freedom, new levels of peace, new levels of opportunity. In this seventh year, what you used to struggle with is not going to be a struggle anymore.

CHAPTER EIGHT

Believing Without a Sign

Where God is taking you, the amazing future He has planned, is going to require you to not be moved by what you don't see, to trust Him when there's no evidence.

We all have dreams and goals, promises we're standing on. When we see God's favor, doors opening, our health improving, the right people showing up, it's easy to believe. We know God is at work. But sometimes we're doing our best, praying and believing, but nothing's happening. The office politics are getting worse, your daughter's marriage is on the edge, your once safe neighborhood is not so safe anymore. There's no sign that it's going to change. It's easy to get discouraged and give up on what we're believing for. But the Scripture says, "Faith is the evidence of things not seen." If you can see it, it doesn't take any faith. If you have the evidence, it's easy to stay encouraged. But to reach your destiny, there will be times when there is no evidence. Every circumstance says, "You'll never get well, never meet the right person, never accomplish your dream. You're no better off than you were a year ago." We think, *God, if You would just give me a sign, if You would just let me know that You're working, if I could just*

> The Scripture says, "Faith is the evidence of things not seen."

see something improving, I could believe. This is when you have to dig down deep and say, "I don't have to have the evidence. I'm not moved by what I see; I'm moved by what I know. God, I know that You are faithful to what You promised."

Just because you don't see a sign doesn't mean God is not working. Don't believe the lies that nothing is happening. In the unseen realm, God is arranging things in your favor, lining up the healing, the right people, the promotion. When you can't see anything happening, God is showing you that He trusts you. You don't have to see everything to keep moving forward. You've matured to the point where you walk by faith and not by sight. Where God is taking you, the amazing future He has planned, is going to require you to believe without a sign, to trust Him when there's no evidence. If you have to see everything to stay encouraged, to see it to keep believing, it will limit how high you can go. You have to pass the test of staying in faith when nothing is improving, thanking God when all the circumstances say it's never going to change.

You may be there right now. You've been praying and believing, but it doesn't seem as though it's doing any good. You don't see any evidence. It can feel like God is on vacation, that He doesn't even hear your prayers. The silence doesn't mean God has forgotten about you. He sees your faithfulness. He sees you doing the right thing when it's hard. When you could have given up, you went the extra mile and kept believing. When you felt like complaining, you kept praising. When every thought said it was never going to happen, you kept thanking God that He was working. Let me encourage you that your time is coming. What God promised you is on the way. Don't get talked out of it. Don't let people, delays, or doubt convince you to give up. Your breakthrough is already on the schedule.

> The silence doesn't mean God has forgotten about you. He sees your faithfulness.

Your miracle has already been set in motion. It seems like nothing is happening, but suddenly it's going to change, suddenly the dream comes to pass, suddenly the right person shows up.

After Jesus rose from the dead, He told Thomas, "Because you've seen Me, you have believed. But blessed are those who have not seen yet believe." You haven't seen it, but you keep believing. God says there's a blessing coming. Because you believe without the evidence, believe without the sign, favor is coming, healing is coming, victory is coming. Don't be a Thomas and say, "God, show me a sign and then I'll believe. When my circumstances improve, I'll stay in faith. When You open this door, I'll know You're working." God is looking for people who believe without a sign. God is looking for people who are not moved by what they don't see, who don't need the evidence to prove to them that God is working.

> God is looking for people who are not moved by what they don't see, who don't need the evidence to prove to them that God is working.

Let Your Sign Be God's Faithfulness

In 2 Kings 20, King Hezekiah became very sick. He was close to death when the prophet Isaiah showed up at the palace. I'm sure he was hoping for good news. *Maybe Isaiah will prophesy that things are about to turn around, that I'm about to get well.* But it wasn't what he was thinking. Isaiah said, "King Hezekiah, I have a word from the Lord for you. God says, 'Set your house in order, for you will surely die.'" Isaiah didn't say, "It's not looking good, King. You might pass. There's a chance you're not going to make it." No, there was no doubt. "This is the end for you, Hezekiah. You will not recover from this illness." Hezekiah could have been depressed, given up on life, but he immediately began to pray as Isaiah walked away. He reminded God of all the good he had done, how he had torn down pagan shrines and removed all the idols. He poured out his heart and asked God in His mercy to spare his life. Before Isaiah left the palace grounds, God changed His mind and told Isaiah to go back and give him this new report. Isaiah said, "Hezekiah, the Lord says He has heard your prayers, and He's going to heal you. In three days, you will get out of this bed, and He will add fifteen years to your life." You can imagine how excited and how overwhelmed Hezekiah was. He just received the amazing promise that this death sentence had been reversed.

But King Hezekiah was like most of us. After the excitement wore off, he started thinking, *How do I know I'm going to get well? I don't look any different. I don't feel any better. Nothing has changed.* Doubts started to come. *Is it really going to happen? Are you sure that's what God said?* Hezekiah said to Isaiah, "What sign will the Lord give me to prove that I'm going to get well?" He was saying, "Isaiah, I appreciate what you've told me. That's encouraging, but I need some evidence. I need to see something, so I'll believe. I need God to prove that He's going to do it." Isaiah said, "All right, God will give you a sign. Do you want the shadow on the sundial to go ten degrees forward or ten degrees backward?" Hezekiah said backward. They watched as the shadow defied the odds and went backward.

God is merciful. Sometimes He'll give you a sign even if you say, "God, prove that You're going to do what You said. I need some evidence. If I don't see something, I'm not going to believe." But here's my point: If you live by this approach, if you're always dependent on a sign, you won't reach the fullness of your destiny. Maybe you're praying for a sign but you're not seeing anything. The sundial is not going backward. The right attitude is: *God, I don't have to have a sign. You don't have to prove to me that You're going to do it. You've already proven to me who You are. You've already made ways where I didn't see*

> **If you're always dependent on a sign, you won't reach the fullness of your destiny.**

a way. You've already opened doors that I couldn't open. You've already defeated giants that were much bigger. You've already broken chains that I could never break. God, I trust You with no evidence. I'm not a Thomas. I don't have to see it to believe it. I'm not a Hezekiah. You don't have to prove to me that You're faithful. You've already shown Yourself faithful.

It's great when you get a sign, but don't rely on a sign. Don't become dependent on seeing and then you'll believe. That doesn't take faith. Your faith kicks in when there's no evidence. Instead of asking God to prove what He's going to do, why don't you turn it around and prove to God who you are? Prove to Him that you're not going to be moved by what you don't see. Prove that you're not going to give up because things aren't changing. Prove that you're going to stand in faith when every circumstance says it's never going to happen.

What's interesting is that right before King Hezekiah got sick, he had just seen the greatest victory of his life. The Assyrian army was coming against him and the people of Judah. Their army was much bigger, more powerful, and had more resources. The night before the Assyrians were going to attack, the angel of the Lord went into their camp and killed 185,000 soldiers. The others took off running for their lives. Hezekiah and the people of Judah were spared. You would think that Hezekiah wouldn't need a sign. He had just seen a supernatural victory. He just saw God show out. But how many times do we forget what God has done? Like Hezekiah, God has shown

> **How many times do we forget what God has done?**

up and turned things around for us. He's healed us, protected us, freed us, promoted us. If you need a sign, look back at the goodness of God in your life. Look back at how He brought you through the illness, how He gave you strength when you didn't think you could go on, how He promoted you when you weren't next in line, how He turned your child around, how He brought someone great into your life to love, how that one good break caused your business to take off. When you need evidence, look back at the faithfulness of God.

Be an Elijah, Not a Hezekiah

This is what the prophet Elijah did. He prophesied that there would be a great famine in Israel because of idolatry in the land, and for three and a half years it had not rained. There was no water, no crops, and the people were barely surviving. When nothing looked any different in the middle of the drought, Elijah showed up and said, "I hear the sound of the abundance of rain." He was so bold that he went and told King Ahab, "This drought is coming to an end. Rain is on the way." When he said that, there wasn't a cloud in the sky. God will put things in your spirit that contradict what you see. He heard an abundance of rain, but he saw barren ground, dried-up crops, drought, and famine. The key is: Don't let what you see override what you've heard. If you're always looking for a sign, you're going to get discouraged. "I heard rain, but I see drought. I heard healing, but I see sickness. I heard abundance, but I see lack. Joel, I heard freedom, but all I see is dysfunction, addictions, and depression. When I see something different, I'll believe. When I have some evidence, I'll get my hopes up."

No, don't be a Hezekiah. Be an Elijah. You don't have to have a sign. God doesn't have to prove to you that He's going to do what He's promised. You've seen His faithfulness. You have a history with Him. He's made things happen all through your life that you could

> **Don't let what you see talk you out of what you've heard in your spirit.**

never have made happen. Now do your part and believe without a sign. Stay in faith when there's no evidence. Don't let what you see talk you out of what you've heard in your spirit. It's very powerful when you can say, "I don't see any sign of what I'm believing for, but that's okay. I don't need a sign. I know God is on the throne. I know He's in control. I know what He started, He will finish."

After declaring to King Ahab that rain was coming, Elijah climbed to the top of Mount Carmel to pray. He bowed down and began to thank God that rain was coming, that what He heard in his spirit was on the way. He asked his assistant to go to the other side of the mountain and see if there was any sign of rain. Elijah wasn't dependent on a sign; he was expecting rain and looking for God's goodness. That's different than saying, "I'm not going to believe unless I have a sign." His attitude was: *I know God is at work. It could happen anytime. I know rain is coming.* He had this confidence, this unshakeable faith. The assistant came back and said, "Sorry, Elijah, but there are no clouds. It's as clear as can be." If he could have checked the latest doppler weather radar, there would have been nothing in sight. Elijah didn't get depressed and say, "God, I must have heard You wrong." No, he kept thanking God that rain was coming. He didn't let the lack of evidence convince him that it wasn't going to happen. He kept looking for the rain, expecting the rain, talking as though the rain was going to happen.

> **He kept looking for the rain, expecting the rain, talking as though the rain was going to happen.**

I can hear King Ahab laughing and saying, "Elijah, where's that rain you were talking about? I thought you said there's going to be an abundance. I haven't felt one little drop." Elijah would have responded, "Ahab, I'm not worried. I don't need a sign to believe. I'm not dependent on the evidence. I know what God has spoken to me will come to pass."

Elijah sent the assistant out again to see if he saw any sign of rain. He came back again and again and again, with the same report—not a cloud in the sky, perfectly clear. Six times, and no sign. Six times, and nothing had changed. Six times, and the same negative report. I can imagine that Elijah had thoughts that said, *It's not going to happen. Just accept it. No rain is coming.* You may be where Elijah was. You know what God has promised you—health, freedom, abundance, a spouse, a child—but you've been looking, standing in faith, thanking God, but there's no evidence. Nothing is improving. There are still no good breaks. This is when you have to dig down deep and say, "God, I'm not moved by what I don't see. I know that You're a faithful God. I'm going to keep looking, keep expecting, keep prais-

> Don't let the clear sky fool you. God can change things suddenly.

ing, keep declaring that it's on the way." Don't let the clear sky fool you. God can change things suddenly. He controls the universe. One touch of His favor, and you'll see the abundance of rain. When you're not seeing any sign of it, that's a test. What are you made of? Are you going to give up, get discouraged, and settle for mediocrity, or are you going to do as Elijah did and keep believing despite what you're seeing?

On the seventh time, the assistant came back and said, "Elijah, this time I saw a small cloud on the horizon, about the size of a man's hand." Soon after that the heavens opened up, there was a huge downpour, and the three-and-a-half-year drought suddenly came to an end. Like Elijah, you have been faithful. You've believed when every circumstance said it wasn't going to happen. You didn't listen to the naysayers, didn't get talked out of it, and you've been looking for God's goodness. I believe you're about to come into your seventh time. You're about to see the open windows of Heaven. You're about to see something better than you've imagined, more rewarding, more fulfilling. The Scripture says, "There was a remarkable rainstorm." God is going to do something remarkable in your life, something out of the ordinary, something that will exceed your expectations.

An Unshakeable Faith

It's significant that Elijah's assistant, someone who was close to him, kept bringing him the news that it wasn't going to happen. "Elijah, there are no clouds." He didn't mean to be negative. He was just reporting the facts. But sometimes the people closest to you will try to talk you out of what God put in your heart. They may mean well, but they didn't hear what God spoke to you. They'll keep telling you what they see. You can't let their negative comments and doubts drown out what you've heard. "Do you still think you're going to get well? It's been a long battle." "Do you really believe your child is going to get back on course? He's doing worse than ever." "Do you think you're going to have a bountiful year? I don't see it in this economy. The gas prices and inflation are setting you back." They're looking at it in the natural, but we serve a supernatural God.

There will be seasons like what Elijah experienced when you're looking, expecting, and believing, but again and again there's no sign, no improvement. What if on the fourth time Elijah would have said to the assistant, "I guess you're right. It's not going to rain." What if on the fifth time he had gotten discouraged and said, "God,

> **What if on the fourth time Elijah would have said to the assistant, "I guess you're right. It's not going to rain."**

I thought I heard You, but surely it should have happened by now. At least I should see some clouds, some wind, some sign that things are about to change." Maybe that's where you are, on your fourth time, with no evidence of change. Then your fifth time, and still no sign. On your sixth time, the sky is still blue. Don't give up now. Those are tests. Yes, it would be much easier if we always got a sign like Hezekiah did. But we'd never grow. We wouldn't reach our potential. Where God is taking you is going to take an unshakeable faith. You won't be moved by what you see or discouraged because of a lack of evidence.

I know that you're not a Thomas who is saying, "Lord, show me and I'll believe." I know that you're not a Hezekiah who is saying, "God, give me a sign and I'll trust You." I know that you're an Elijah who is saying, "God, I believe without a sign." You keep looking for rain even though your skies are clear. You don't let people, how long it's been, delays, or what's not happening talk you out of what you've heard in your spirit. You are headed for an abundance of rain, an abundance of joy, an abundance of favor, an abundance of resources. You are headed for something remarkable, uncommon, that will take your family to a new level.

> You are headed for an abundance of rain, an abundance of joy, an abundance of favor, an abundance of resources.

Your Seventh Time Is Coming

Right after we acquired our church facility, the former Compaq Center, a huge real estate company that owned all the property around the building filed a lawsuit to try to keep us from moving in. We had just come off this great victory, only to find out that it was now tied up in the courts and we couldn't move forward. Our attorneys told us that it could take up to ten years to settle. They had met with the other side, but they were in no hurry to do something. In fact, the more they delayed, the more at a disadvantage we were. Our main attorney called and said, "Joel, they're playing hardball. They don't want to talk or negotiate. They're stubborn." A month went by, and nothing happened. Two months...three months...four months... five months, and nothing. Not a cloud in the sky. No evidence that it was ever going to work out. I had to do what I'm asking you to do. I just kept thanking God. "Father, I'm not moved by what I don't see. I don't need a sign. I'm not looking for evidence. I know that when it's Your time, all the forces of darkness cannot stop what You have ordained for us."

Doubt tried to come, negative thoughts came, and some people tried to talk us out of it. Our main attorney asked me, "What if I got them to give you enough funds to build a facility like this somewhere else?" I told him, "We don't want somewhere else." This building is a landmark in Houston. Two million Houstonians had come to this building every year for thirty years. Don't let a lack of evidence cause you to water down your dreams. Don't settle for mediocrity. What God has for you is going to take resilience, determination, and perseverance. You have to have a made-up mind. You can't be talked out of it. You can't be moved by what you see. What you see may contradict what God put in your heart. You may not see anything improving. I didn't see the other side letting up. I didn't see any sign of progress. Like Elijah, we heard no for a third time, a fourth time, and a fifth time. There was no evidence of budging, no movement at all. But if you stay in faith, you're going to come into your seventh time when things suddenly

> What God has for you is going to take resilience, determination, and perseverance. You have to have a made-up mind.

change. Suddenly the door opens. Suddenly the wrong people are moved out of the way. Suddenly your health begins to turn around.

Unexpectedly, one day almost two years later, our attorney said the other side had called and wanted to meet. He said, "Joel, don't get your hopes up. This is probably just a ploy to distract us." He didn't realize my hopes had already been up. For two years, I had been thanking God, looking for His goodness, expecting His favor. When we met the CEO of the company, the first thing he said was, "Joel, I watch you on television every week, and my son-in-law is a youth pastor." God knows how to bring the right people at the right time. Twenty-four hours later, he had agreed to let us have the building and to lease us nine thousand covered parking spaces so we didn't have to build a garage.

You may not see any sign of what you're believing for. You could get discouraged and let the lack of evidence talk you out of it. No, stay in faith. God is working behind the scenes. You may be on your fourth time or your fifth time. This is not the time to give up. You are closer than you think. Your seventh time is coming. It's going to happen suddenly. It's going to be supernatural, something that you couldn't make happen.

The truth is that CEO could have shown up two years earlier. If he had, I wouldn't have had to pray and believe and trust. But it's the times when we have to wait, believe, and not be moved by what we don't see that are preparing us for the new levels God has in store. Don't get discouraged because it's not happening on your timetable. Everything is serving God's plan. When you're waiting, staying in faith, believing when there's no sign, you're growing. You're showing God what you're made of. Instead of God proving to you who He is, you're

> It's the times when we have to wait, believe, and not be moved by what we don't see that are preparing us for the new levels God has in store.

proving to Him who you are. Anybody can get discouraged. Anybody can be a Thomas and say, "I'm not going to believe unless I see it." But God is looking for Elijahs who aren't moved by the lack of evidence, who don't water down their dreams, who believe without a sign.

Your Faithfulness Will Be Rewarded

When my father was seventeen years old, God put a dream in his heart that one day he would pastor a church with thousands of people. He had been raised very poor, but he dared to leave the farm. In 1959, he and my mother started Lakewood on Mother's Day with ninety people. He eventually named the church Lakewood International Outreach Center. The fact is, it was a small neighborhood church, but he called it an international outreach. That dream was still alive. But for thirteen years, Lakewood barely grew. It had less than two hundred people. My father knew what God had spoken to him, a church with thousands, but there was no evidence. He could have gotten discouraged and said, "God, show me a sign. Let me know that it's going to happen." But year after year, my father and mother just kept being faithful and ministering to the people, thanking God that what my father heard in his spirit was on the way. It would be so much easier if we saw a good break, a little growth, the right person showing up. But sometimes God will withhold the evidence. He's seeing what we're going to do. Are we going to be a Thomas? "God, I'll believe and give it my best if You show me a sign." God is giving you an opportunity to grow, to trust Him in a greater way, to prove to Him that you'll walk by faith and not by sight so He can entrust you with more.

In 1972, it was as though God opened a faucet and people started coming to Lakewood from all over the city. Lakewood grew from a church of a couple hundred to many thousands. My father saw what God put in his spirit. God could have done that the first year or the second year, but we have to pass these tests. We all go through silent seasons when we're believing and praying, but nothing is changing. You don't see any sign that what God promised is going to happen. You'll be tempted to walk away from a dream, to give up on a child, a spouse, or a breakthrough. "God, if You just do what You did for Hezekiah and prove that You're going to do it, I'll start believing again."

But most of the time it's going to be like what Elijah went through. No sign. People saying it's not going to happen. Your thoughts telling you it's never going to rain. Do as he did. Don't be moved by what you see. The skies may be clear right now, but your seventh time is coming. God sees your faithfulness. He sees you believing when there's no evidence. You are closer than you think. The clouds are starting to form right now. I believe and declare your abundance of rain is on the way. What you're believing for is going to happen suddenly, unexpectedly. Healing, favor, and breakthroughs are on the way.

> **You are closer than you think. The clouds are starting to form right now.**

CHAPTER NINE

Pray for Others

**There are people God has put in your life who won't
become all they were created to be without you praying
and moving the hands that rule the world.**

It's good to pray for yourself, pray for your dreams, pray for wisdom, to ask God to help you overcome difficulties. That's important, but don't stop there. You have the ability to help someone else reach their destiny. There are people God has put in your life who won't become all they were created to be without you praying. They don't have the faith to accomplish their dreams. They won't overcome the challenge without you stepping up and asking God to help them. The Scripture tells us, "Pray for one another." You don't have to go to them and make a big deal about it. I'm talking about you taking some time every day to pray privately for others, and not to just focus on your dreams, your needs, your goals. Look around at who God has put in your life. It may be a neighbor who seems down, or a coworker who's struggling, or someone you heard about who's fighting cancer. They didn't come up by accident. God brought them across your path. He's counting on you to lift them up.

"Joel, I'm dealing with my own problems, my own dreams, my own issues. I need somebody to pray for me." When you pray for others, you're sowing a seed for God to help you. In the Old Testament, even when Job was overcome with all kinds of challenges and his whole world had fallen apart, he understood this principle. He didn't just pray for himself; he prayed for his friends. He turned his focus away from his own needs and prayed for others. The Scripture says, "When Job prayed for his friends, the Lord restored his health."

> Could it be that if you would take time to pray for others, what you're struggling with would turn around?

Could it be that if you would take time to pray for others, what you're struggling with would turn around? Then your health, your dream, or your breakthrough would show up.

The apostle Paul says, "Bear one another's burdens." We weren't meant to carry the load on our own. We need one another. Life can be heavy. Some people are lonely and others have been through disappointments. They're dealing with illnesses. They can smile on the outside but be hurting inside. They have pressure and stress that we know nothing about. When you pray for them, it helps lighten the load. Your prayer causes the angels to go to work. Chains that have held them back begin to loosen. When you speak faith into their destiny, the forces of darkness that are trying to sour their future with depression, sickness, and loneliness begin to lose their grip. It may not happen overnight, but your prayer is making a difference. Your prayer may be what's keeping them going. They don't even know you're praying, and you may not get any credit. But the Scripture says that what you do in secret, God will reward you in the open. When you pray for others, God will always make sure somebody is praying for you.

Silence in Heaven

When I meet people, many of them say, "Joel, you've helped and encouraged me. I like listening to you." That's all good, and I

> **Prayer moves the hands that rule the world.**

appreciate hearing that. But my favorite thing is when they say, "Joel, I'm praying for you." When you pray for someone, you're not just giving them good wishes. You're not just saying, "Good luck. I hope all goes well for you." Prayer moves the hands that rule the world. Prayer causes the God who created the universe to make things happen that we couldn't make happen. When you pray, all of Heaven comes to attention.

In the book of Revelation, John described what he saw in Heaven, how the angels around the throne are constantly singing and worshipping, saying, "Holy, holy, holy is the Lord God, the Almighty." But in Chapter 8, he wrote that there was silence in Heaven for about half an hour. During that time an angel came to the altar with a golden censer of incense, which represents the prayers coming from the Earth. The Scripture says, "The smoke of the incense, together with the prayers of the saints, went up before God." Notice how powerful prayer is.

> **What could be so important that all of Heaven came to a standstill?**

In Heaven, there was all this singing, all this worship, but suddenly the angels stopped singing, the heavenly host were silenced. What could be so important that all of Heaven came to a standstill? Was something wrong, was there an emergency? No, Heaven stopped to hear the prayers of God's people. It makes a difference when you pray. Your prayers go up like incense before the throne of God.

It may feel as though nobody's listening when you pray. Thoughts whisper, *You're wasting your time. God is not concerned about you.* No, just imagine that when you pray, the angels get quiet and the musicians stop playing. Gabriel says to God, "I've silenced everything because I see a prayer is coming up. Somebody is asking You for a favor. Somebody believes You can do the impossible. Somebody is counting on You to break an addiction, to turn a child around, to heal a friend of cancer." When you pray, something powerful happens. All of Heaven stops, and the Creator of the universe comes to attention. That's when supernatural things take place. When you pray, Red Seas part, Goliaths are defeated, hungry lions can't open their mouths, Compaq Centers show up, cancer is overcome, and blessings rain down. I'm asking you to not just pray for yourself, but pray for others. Use that power to help somebody else reach their destiny.

See People as a Peter

In Acts 12, King Herod Agrippa was against the church. He not only had the believers arrested, but he had the apostle James killed. When he saw how that pleased the people, he was planning to do the same thing to the apostle Peter. They arrested Peter and put him in prison. He was in the deepest dungeon, the most secure place, with chains on both wrists. He was guarded by four squads of soldiers. They took extra precautions to make sure Peter didn't get out. The night before he was going to go to trial, it says, "The church was earnestly praying for Peter." The believers had all gathered at a house, and they spent the night praying for their friend, asking God to make a way, to somehow bring him out. While they were praying in the middle of the night, an angel showed up in the prison and woke Peter up. Peter wasn't praying; he was asleep. Maybe he thought it was too late, maybe he was too discouraged to pray, but he had friends who were praying. The chains fell off Peter's wrists. The angel and Peter walked past the first set of guards and they didn't notice, then past the second set. When they came to the big iron gate, it opened of its own accord. Peter's life was spared.

What's interesting is that the Scripture specifically mentions that the church was praying for Peter, but it doesn't mention anyone had been praying for James. They were in the same situation but had opposite results. Peter's life was spared while James lost his. While we rejoice over what God did for Peter, I wonder if James wouldn't have been killed if people had been praying for him as they did for Peter. Maybe the angel would have showed up for James and the prison doors would have opened. Maybe God would have changed Herod's mind if somebody had been praying. My challenge is, don't let there be a James in your life. Don't let your family, your children, your coworkers, or your neighbors be a James. All your family, friends, and relatives should be Peters. Cover them in prayer. Ask God to strengthen them, to protect them, to heal them, to show them favor. Pray that they will accomplish their dreams. Pray that they will make their mark on this generation. Your prayer can make the difference. Your prayer can cause God to send the angel.

> All your family, friends, and relatives should be Peters. Cover them in prayer.

When you believe for favor on their behalf, when you ask God to make a way for them, Heaven comes to attention. God is concerned about what concerns you. They may not have the faith to believe for themselves. They may not be living right and don't deserve favor, but because you're honoring God, because you took the time to ask, God will bless them for your sake. You've been given a gift. You can help somebody else succeed. On their own, they can't do it. On their own, they are a James, but with your prayer, the prison door will open, the addiction will be broken, the right people will show up to help. Are you using your gift? Are you praying for others? Life is too short for you to live self-centered, only thinking about your

> Are you using your gift? Are you praying for others?

needs, your goals, your dreams. That's a shallow way to live. You'll never be truly fulfilled that way because you need other people standing in faith with you. If you develop this habit of praying for others, God will make sure there will always be plenty of people praying for you. The Scripture says, "One can chase a thousand but two can put ten thousand to flight." You are ten times more powerful when somebody is praying for you.

Every morning when I pray, I take time to pray for everyone who's reading my books, for everyone who's a part of our ministry, for your dreams, for your goals, for restoration, for healing, for abundance. Some nights before I go to bed, I go into my backyard and pray for all the people who are hurting in the world. I don't know them by name, but God does. Whenever my brother, Paul, gets back from his overseas mission trips where he's been operating on disadvantaged people who have experienced so much heartache and pain, I pray for them. I believe God brought these people across my path through my brother, not just to feel sorry for them, not just to say that's too bad for them, but to say, "God, show them Your mercy, protect them, heal the hurts, let them see Your goodness." How do you know that your prayer isn't going to protect a child from danger, to keep an accident from happening to a friend, or to lift the burden off a family that's endured incredible pain?

> How do you know that your prayer isn't going to protect a child from danger, to keep an accident from happening to a friend, or to lift the burden off a family that's endured incredible pain?

Recently, an older man, a foreigner, who was very nicely dressed, came up to me on the street. He told me that he and his family had learned about God through watching our program, and that it helped them to overcome some tough times. I was grateful and thanked him for telling me. As I was leaving, I said almost in passing, "I'm going to be praying for you." Then I saw these big tears start to roll down his cheeks. He said so genuinely, "Why would you pray for me? You don't even know me. I don't come from the same faith background." I said, "None of that matters. I don't just pray for people who are like me. I know that God brought you across my path." You don't meet people by accident. God puts people in our lives and brings them to our attention. Maybe it's somebody at the grocery store who looks lonely. Don't see them as a James; see them as a Peter. Under your breath, say, "God, bless them, strengthen them, help them live in victory."

Stand in the Gap

For many years, my mother prayed for an entertainer in our city named Bill Nash. She would see his name on marquees of different clubs. Driving to church each week, she'd see his name again and again. My mother had never met him, but she had read that when he was growing up, his parents were missionaries. He came from a strong family of faith, but in his teens he started running with the wrong people and ended up abusing drugs and alcohol. Instead of singing in churches as he did growing up, he started singing in the clubs. My mother could have dismissed it and thought, *Too bad that he's off course, but it's none of my business.* Instead, every time she saw his name, she would pray, "Lord, help him to get back on course. Help him to fulfill his destiny." Just a simple prayer. This went on year after year. It didn't look as though anything was happening and she was wasting her breath. But when you pray, things are changing. The miracle is set in motion. You may not see anything happening, but God is working. Those prayers have gone up like incense before the throne.

> **When you pray, things are changing. The miracle is set in motion.**

One Sunday morning, Bill was flipping through TV channels and heard my father talking about how God is full of mercy, how He's bigger than any mistakes we've made. That same Sunday, Bill showed up at Lakewood. He sat in the very back. Somebody recognized him and told my mother. She went back, gave him a hug, and told him that she'd been praying for him for years. That day was a turning point. Bill recommitted his life to Christ. A few months later, he held his first Christian concert at Lakewood, and he's been using his talents for the Lord ever since. Today, he and his wife, Kim, have an outreach to help teenagers stay on track. Maybe that wouldn't have happened if my mother had not prayed. Maybe he would still be struggling, still be off course, if she hadn't come before God on his behalf.

The Scripture calls this standing in the gap for people. Some people are too off course to get back on their own. They're too discouraged. They have too many obstacles. It's going to take someone who will go to God on their behalf. In Ezekiel 22, God said, "I looked for someone who would build up the wall and stand in the gap on behalf of the land so I would not have to destroy it, but I found none." Back in those days, cities had walls around them to protect them from enemies. At times, there would be a broken place in the wall, something happened that caused a gap. The enemy could easily come in. So they would place an armed soldier, one of their strongest warriors, to stand in the gap until they could get the wall repaired.

People all around us have broken-down walls. Like Bill Nash, they've gotten off course. Perhaps a relationship didn't work out, or they're fighting an illness, depression, and loneliness. There's a breach in their wall. God is asking you, "Will you stand in the gap? Will you cover them while they're down? Will you not let the enemy overtake them?"

> "Will you stand in the gap? Will you cover them while they're down? Will you not let the enemy overtake them?"

When my father died and I stepped up to pastor the church, my wall was broken down. I thought, *How is this ever going to work out?* But I could feel people praying for me. I could tell people were standing in the gap. When I couldn't do it on my own, I had many members of our church who were covering me, praying for me, speaking faith into my destiny until I could get that wall repaired. I am where I am today because people stood in the gap for me. Like me, you've had people stand in the gap for you. What's been given to us, we have a responsibility to give to others. Let's be people who are quick to stand in the gap. When somebody around you has a broken-down wall, life hasn't turned out the way they thought. They're hurting, they're lonely, and they don't think they can go on. That's your cue to step up and make a difference. Don't just feel sorry for them. Pray for them. Ask God to lighten the load. When you pray, Heaven listens.

> **Don't just feel sorry for them. Pray for them.**

The twenty-year-old daughter of a family that attends Lakewood recently had an aneurysm and suddenly died. The father told me with tears, "I don't think I can go on. The pain isn't letting up." His wall was down; there'd been a breach. Yes, I felt sorry; yes, it broke my heart. But feeling sorry is not enough. That's when you have to make it your mission to stand in the gap. Every morning you have to say, "Lord, strengthen that family, heal their wounds, give them beauty for ashes." When you stand in the gap, you're not only protecting them from forces that are trying to get in, such as depression and hopelessness, but God will use you to bring healing and restoration.

Be the Difference Maker

After all God had done for the Israelites, delivering them from slavery in Egypt, parting the Red Sea, and giving them food in the desert, they got off course. At one point, they started worshipping a golden calf, having wild parties where they were getting drunk and being immoral. God was so angry that He was going to destroy them, but Moses went up on the mountain and for forty days fasted and prayed, asking God for His mercy—not for himself, but for the Israelites. It says in Psalm 106, "God would have destroyed them had not Moses stood in the gap before Him." You may have family members,

> **Because one man stood in the gap for them, God changed His mind.**

friends, and coworkers who are off course and making poor choices. They know better, but they're doing it anyway. That's where the Israelites were. God was ready to destroy them, some two million people, but because one man stood in the gap for them, God changed His mind.

Why don't you do like Moses and stand in the gap for the people who are not doing right. It's easy to criticize them, to write them off. You can be the one who makes a difference. I want the psalmist to be able to put my name or your name in that scripture. God would have destroyed them had not Robert stood in the gap, had not Marie stood in the gap, had not Julie stood in the gap. I've found that if you're not standing in the gap for someone, you're probably standing in judgment. I've made up my mind that I'm going to live my life as a gap stander. I'm going to be a people lifter. I'm going to take time every day to help pray people into their destiny.

In Chapter Four, I mentioned that this is exactly what the Roman centurion whom Jesus marveled at for his great faith did in Luke 7. When his servant was sick and in so much pain, close to death, the centurion asked Jesus to heal his slave. This respected, influential man was standing in the gap for someone who most people back then would have written off. They bought and sold slaves all the time. But this commander was different. He loved this servant and couldn't sleep at night thinking that he was in pain. I can imagine that when he started heading out to see Jesus, people asked him, "Why are you going? Do you need a miracle? Do you need healing? Is something wrong with you?" The centurion replied, "No, I'm going on behalf of my slave." He was standing in the gap for "the least of these." He was standing in the gap for somebody who was looked down on, somebody who had no influence, somebody whom society said was not important.

As we saw previously, Jesus said about this centurion, "I have not seen such faith in all of Israel," then He spoke and the servant was healed. What's interesting is that this centurion wasn't a Jew; he didn't come from the same faith. Yet Jesus said this Gentile had more faith than all the people who were around him. God is not looking at how religious you are, at what church you attend, or how you were raised. What gets His attention is when you're concerned about the less fortunate. When you stand in the gap for the least of these, for those who don't have the opportunity that you do, for those who have been dealt an unfair hand, God calls that great faith.

> **When you stand in the gap for the least of these, for those who don't have the opportunity that you do, for those who have been dealt an unfair hand, God calls that great faith.**

Make Prayer Your Priority

In the Scripture, Joseph was falsely accused of a crime and put into an Egyptian prison. After he had been imprisoned for many years, Joseph was joined by Pharaoh's butler and baker, who had offended the ruler. The butler had a dream one night, and Joseph was able to interpret it. He told the butler that he was going to get out of prison and be restored to his position. The butler was so excited and so grateful. Joseph said, "Do me a favor. When you get out, please remind Pharaoh that I'm here and I haven't done anything to deserve being in this dungeon." Just as Joseph said, the butler got out and was restored to his position, but the butler forgot all about how Joseph helped him. Now when Joseph needed help, the butler was nowhere to be found. All of us have been where this butler was. Somebody helped us, somebody gave us a good break, somebody encouraged us when we were down, somebody prayed when we were sick. They stood in the gap for us. Now don't be like this butler; stand in the gap for somebody else. You're blessed, so be a blessing. God answered your prayers; now pray for somebody else.

The truth is that none of us got to where we are by ourselves. I had parents who prayed over me, who spoke faith into my destiny. I'm seeing God's favor because somebody stood in the gap for me. My siblings and I never left the house for school in the morning without my mother praying for favor and protection. Now, I not only pray for my children, but I pray for my grandchildren who are not even here yet. I pray for my great grandchildren. When my descendants show up, they may not realize it, but they've already been covered in prayer. They're going to see favor, good breaks, and mercy because I've taken time to pray. David's son Solomon got into trouble, made poor choices, and God was going to take his throne away. But then God said to Solomon, "For the sake of your father, David, I will show you mercy and not do it." That's how powerful it is when you not only live a life that honors God, but you take time to pray for your children, pray for your descendants.

As a little girl, Victoria used to go to her grandmother's house

> **The truth is that none of us got to where we are by ourselves.**

in Georgia. When she would wake up early, before anyone else was awake, she would see her grandmother out under a tree, praying on her knees. She was covering her family, covering her children, covering her seed in prayer. Victoria never dreamed that she would be in the ministry. We never dreamed we'd be this blessed, this fulfilled. It's because people took time to pray for us. Somebody did it for us, and somebody did it for you, so let's do it for somebody else. Look around at who is in your life. Are there some Jameses—people who aren't going to reach their destiny without your prayers? I'm asking you to turn them into Peters. Make it your mission to pray for them. Stand in the gap. Ask God to bless them. If you do this, I believe and declare that the seed you sow is going to come back to you. As you pray for others like Job did, you're going to see your prayers answered, your healing come, and your dreams fulfilled.

> Are there some Jameses—people who aren't going to reach their destiny without your prayers?

CHAPTER TEN

Keep Believing for Your Loved Ones

God is counting on you to give people room to change, to show them mercy and encourage them, not to judge them or to find fault, but to stand in the gap and pray for them.

We all have someone in our life who we hope will change. It may be a family member who's off course, a child who's not making good decisions, a friend who's gotten in trouble with the law. We're praying and believing, but it doesn't look like it's making any difference. It's easy to get frustrated and think we're wasting our time. But if they're going to reach their destiny, they need someone who will wait on them. They need someone who will keep praying, keep encouraging, keep speaking faith into their future. "You may be struggling with an addiction, running with the wrong crowd, and compromising, but that is not who you are. Freedom is on the way. I still believe in you. I know that you have seeds of greatness. The hand of God is on your life." They need someone who will stand in the gap and believe for them when they can't believe for themselves. They need someone who will cover them with mercy, not judge them, not condemn them, but will help love them back into wholeness.

We write off people too easily. Where they are now is not where they're going to end up. Don't judge them by the present. Before the apostle Paul was a follower of Christ, before he wrote almost half the books of the New Testament, his name was Saul and he hated believers. He was the biggest enemy of the church. He went from city to city having believers arrested and even killed. If you and I had seen him, we would have thought, *This guy doesn't have a chance. He's a terrorist. He's against everything we stand for.* Yet God told a disciple in Damascus named Ananias, "Go pray for Saul. He is a chosen vessel to bear My name." Some of the people we're tempted to write off are chosen vessels. They're going to advance the kingdom and do great things. All they need is for someone to wait on them. They need someone to say, "Yes, they're pretty far out, but I'm going to send them a text and tell them that I'm praying for them. I'm going to invite them to lunch, not condemn them or try to straighten them out. I'm going to tell them that I love them, that I believe in them, and that if they need anything, all they have to do is ask." Will you wait on someone while God is changing them?

> **Some of the people we're tempted to write off are chosen vessels.**

The God Who Waits on Us

In Chapter One, we looked briefly at Jesus meeting the Samaritan woman at a well. When Jesus asked her to give Him a drink of water, she was surprised because normally Jews would have nothing to do with Samaritans. Jesus answered, "If you knew who I am, you would ask Me and I would give you living water." She replied, "Please, sir, give me this water." Jesus told her to go and call her husband. When she explained that she didn't have a husband, Jesus said, "You're right. The fact is, you've had five husbands, and the man you now have is not your husband." She responded, "You must be a prophet. We know one day the Messiah will come." Jesus looked at her and said, "I am the Messiah." She went home and told everyone in the town what happened. The Scripture says that many Samaritans from that town believed in Jesus because of this woman's testimony.

What's interesting is that Jesus could have gone into the city with His disciples to get food. He was hungry, but He chose to wait at the well. Notice who He was waiting for—a woman who didn't have a good reputation. He waited for a woman who had been married five times and was living with another man, a woman who had blown it. I'm sure people had written her off and thought, *She is so messed up.* When she walked by, I imagine people whispered, "There's that woman. I wonder who she's living with this week." People would laugh and gossip about her. It's easy to fault her and think, *She must have been loose. Something must have been wrong with her.* The truth is that this lady had been rejected by men and pushed down again and again.

> **Jesus waited for a woman who felt like a failure, who had little self-worth, who had low self-esteem, who didn't feel valuable.**

Jesus waited for a woman who felt like a failure, who had little self-worth, who had low self-esteem, who didn't feel valuable.

You would think Jesus would have waited for the mayor of the city, for someone with prominence and influence. Jesus was busy. He had all kinds of demands, people pulling on Him and wanting His help, but He chose to wait for a woman who didn't have it all together. He didn't judge her. He didn't find fault. He spoke life into her. He lifted her. He valued her. It's significant that the Samaritans embraced a religion that was a mixture of Judaism and idolatry. Jesus waited for a woman who came from a different faith. The first person Jesus ever told He was the Messiah was not a religious leader, not the chief priest. When He wanted to announce one of the most important things He would ever say, He said it to this woman. Society said, "Forget about her. She's a reject. She makes bad choices." But God said, "I'm not only going to wait on her, I'm going to honor her by telling her who I am."

Think about how many times God waited on us. He waited when we were off course. He waited when we had a bad attitude. He waited when we failed, when we were addicted and compromising. He could have said, "That's it. I'm done with you." But He waited. He showed us mercy. He picked us up when we fell. He kept the addiction from taking our life. He protected us when we chose the wrong friends. He stopped the accident that could have taken us out. He waited when we didn't believe in Him. He waited when we were bitter because He didn't answer our prayer. He waited when we ignored Him. Sometimes you need to look back and say, "Lord, thank You for waiting on me. Thank You for giving me another chance. Thank You for cleaning up the mess I made. Thank You for covering me when I didn't deserve it."

> **Think about how many times God waited on us.**

Pray Them Back

God has waited on all of us. Now He's asking us, "Will you wait on someone for Me? Will you wait on your friend who's making bad choices? Will you call them, encourage them, and let them know that you care? Will you wait on your neighbor who doesn't believe in Me, who makes fun of your faith? Will you stand in the gap for them, keep letting your light shine? Will you wait on your relative who's been off course for years, struggling with addictions?" Perhaps it's seemed that the more you pray, the worse he gets. You're ready to give up. No, God is saying, "Wait on him. Keep praying, keep encouraging, and keep loving."

The writer of Proverbs says, "Train up a child in the way they should go, and when they are old, they will not depart from it." You may have a child who's off course. The good news is that you trained them up to know the Lord. That faith was deposited in their spirit. The promise is that in the end, they will not depart from it. It doesn't say anything about the middle. They may take some wrong turns. There may be times when it doesn't look like they're ever going to get back on track. Wait on them. Keep believing, keep encouraging, and keep praying. "Joel, they won't listen. They don't take my advice. They won't return my calls." Don't get discouraged. God knows how to get their attention. You keep praying, and something is happening. In the end, they will not depart. They're off course now, but your declaration should be, "They're coming back. As for me and my house, we will serve the Lord."

> Wait on them. Keep believing, keep encouraging, and keep praying.

You don't have to force them to change. When they're grown, you can't make them do what's right. Don't always try to correct them, threaten them, or give them a lesson. Sometimes you just have to love them. The Scripture says, "Love never fails." You can love them back on track. Love them when they don't deserve it. Love them when they don't listen. Love them when they're making bad decisions. It's easy to write them off and think, *You know better. I'm not going to have anything to do with you.* No, God waited on you, and you have to wait on them.

> "Love never fails." You can love them back on track. Love them when they don't deserve it. Love them when they don't listen.

By Your Love

In the story of the prodigal son in Luke 15, the young man took his father's inheritance, left home, and wasted it all living wildly and partying. He got so desperate that he was living in a hog pen. He decided to go back home and see if he could get a job working as a hired servant in his father's house. The Scripture says, "When his father saw him a long way off, he ran toward his son." Notice that the father was waiting. I can imagine several times a day he'd go out to the end of the driveway and look for his son. "Lord, thank You that my son is coming home. Thank You that You're protecting him. Thank You that he'll fulfill his destiny." He ran out and hugged his son. He told his staff, "We're going to have a party and celebrate the fact that my son is back home." Never once did the father bring up the son's faults. He didn't give an "I told you so" speech. He didn't condemn him and say, "I'll let you stay, but you don't deserve it." He was full of mercy.

I've learned that everyone is on a journey. Where they are now is not where they're going to be in ten years. Give them room to change. They may not believe as you believe. They may have different views. Just keep loving them. Sometimes we think we have to convict people, tell them everything they're doing wrong, and change their mind. But the Holy Spirit is the One who convicts and changes minds. Our job is to just plant the seed. That seed may fall on hard ground. Their heart may not be open. But the good news is, the seed never dies. I read that researchers found a 2,000-year-old Judean date palm seed recovered from excavations at Herod the Great's palace in Israel. When they planted the seed, it came to life and grew into a full plant. All it needed was the right soil. The

> Everyone is on a journey. Where they are now is not where they're going to be in ten years. Give them room to change.

seeds you plant in people's hearts are still alive. The soil may not be ready yet, but at the right time God will soften their heart.

Some people listen to me who don't believe in God, and some come from other faiths. That never bothers me. I'm just sowing seeds, telling people that God is for them, that they're made in His image, that they have a purpose and destiny. I'm telling them that they can overcome their addictions, they can let go of their pasts, and they can reach their God-given dreams. At the right time, those seeds are going to take root. Don't judge others by where they are. They're in the process of changing.

I know a young lady who had been raised in another country and brought up in a different religion. But she liked watching us on television, and she said the messages helped her. She moved to Houston for work and started attending Lakewood, sitting way up at the top. This was all new to her. She expected to hear about how wrong her religion was and to be condemned for how she had been raised, but she never heard any of that. She heard about the goodness of God, how her sins had already been forgiven, and how she could live an abundant life. She eventually gave her life to Christ. She said, "I come from a different faith, and it took two years for me to make my journey to Jesus." You know why that happened? We waited on her. We didn't judge or condemn her. We didn't say, "Be like us or you're out." We gave her room to change. You have to give people time to become who they were created to be.

> You have to give people time to become who they were created to be.

Too often we try to cram things down people's throats and make them believe, but some things don't happen overnight. Will you wait on your friend? Will you keep encouraging your family member even though they're not changing as fast as you would like? Will you wait on your neighbor who doesn't believe? Will you keep sowing seeds of love and kindness, keep being good to them? Jesus says, "By this everyone will know that you are My disciples, by your love for one another." It's not by your doctrine, not by how many scriptures you can quote, not by how right you are, but by how much you love them. You don't judge them. You don't look down on them because they don't believe as you do. You just keep loving them. Keep being good to them.

Show Mercy

A lady told me that she had struggled with her faith for her whole life. One day, her daughter was in an accident and rushed to the hospital. The daughter was injured, but it wasn't serious and she was going to be fine. Later that night, the mother returned home, feeling stressed and overwhelmed by such a difficult day, frustrated and upset. Sitting in her driveway, she looked up and said, "God, why did You do this to me?" At that moment, she said she heard the most loving voice, not out loud but in her heart, say, "That was the first time you've ever spoken to Me." Then she felt a love like she'd never felt, a peace that she'd never experienced. It was the goodness of God overwhelming her.

The Scripture says, "If you draw close to God, He'll draw close to you." We think that if you don't want anything to do with God, He'll say, "Fine. I'll blow you off, too. See if I ever help you." God is not like that. He's as close as the breath you breathe. All you have to do is call out, and He's right there. He's not holding the past against you. He's not upset because you ignored Him. He's not turned off because you don't believe in Him. He's waiting for you. His arms are opened wide. He's at the end of the driveway like that prodigal's father, looking and thinking, *Maybe today you'll come home. Maybe today will be the turning point.*

Are you writing off someone because they don't believe, because they're not making good decisions, because they're against what you stand for? That's where Saul was before he became the apostle Paul. Why don't you start waiting on them, sowing seeds of love, showing mercy instead of judgment? It's easy to have a "holier than thou" attitude. *I can't believe what they're doing! What are they thinking?* If it wasn't for the grace of God, you don't know what you would do. The longer I live, the less judgmental I am. I realize that everybody didn't get what I got. Everyone wasn't raised in a healthy environment, in a home filled with faith and love, with parents who spoke victory over me, with friends and teachers and family who guided me and encouraged me. It's hard enough to succeed when you have all these positive things going for you, but some people come out of family dysfunction, parents who were addicted, depressed, and angry. All they've seen is mediocrity and compromise. It's tempting to look down on them and judge them, but we could have made the same decisions if we were in their shoes. In fact, they may be doing better than we would do in the same circumstances. Instead of finding fault and talking about them, why don't you use that time to pray for them? They're in your life because God is counting on you to help them change. If you wait on them, if you encourage them and be their friend, speak faith into them, they'll step into their destiny. Every seed you sow will come back to you. The mercy you show others is the mercy people will show you.

> Are you writing off someone because they don't believe, because they're not making good decisions, because they're against what you stand for?

> Instead of finding fault and talking about them, why don't you use that time to pray for them?

Sometimes we're waiting for people to change, then we'll accept them. When they start doing right, we'll have a better opinion of them. But God doesn't ask us to clean ourselves up and then we can come to Him. He says, "Come just as you are, and I'll help you get cleaned up." God waited for us when we were off course. He showed us mercy when we were far from our best. Now we need to take that same mercy and show it to someone else.

The Goodness of God

One day, Jesus was traveling through the city of Jericho. Word quickly spread that He was there, and the crowds gathered. Everyone wanted to see Jesus. They had heard about all the miracles and the amazing things He had done. Now the streets were so packed that you could barely move. A man named Zacchaeus, the chief tax collector who was despised for being dishonest and cheating people, wanted to see Jesus, but he was very short. In order to see over everyone, he climbed up in a tree and got in perfect position. As Jesus came walking by, the crowd of people was shouting and waving, trying to get His attention. Suddenly Jesus stopped, looked up in the tree, and said, "Zacchaeus, come down. I want to go to your house and have dinner with you."

What's interesting is the name Zacchaeus means "pure one." In front of all these people who hated Zacchaeus and knew he was a fraud, Jesus called him "Pure One." The principle is that you have to call people what they can become before they'll ever change. The Scripture says, "Call things that are not as if they were." If you keep calling your daughter "Disrespectful," she'll stay disrespectful. If you keep calling your son "Addicted," he'll stay addicted. You're prophesying their future. Change what

> **You have to call people what they can become before they'll ever change.**

you're calling people. Call your child "Blessed," call him "Disciplined," call him "Focused," call him "Successful." That friend who's addicted, start calling him "Free," "Whole," and "Victorious."

Jesus could have said to Zacchaeus, "Hey, you. Hey, tax collector." On purpose, He spoke "Pure One" not only so all the people would hear it, but so Zacchaeus would hear it. Everything got so quiet that you could hear a pin drop. All the eyes turned up to Zacchaeus. I can imagine he nearly passed out. He asked, "Did Jesus just call my name?" Someone shook their head yes. He thought, *How did He know my name?* Sometimes we think that people are so far off course, making such bad choices, that God would never have anything to do with them. The truth is, God knows their name. He's coming after them.

> Sometimes we think that people are so far off course, making such bad choices, that God would never have anything to do with them.

There were city leaders, temple priests, and elders from the synagogue in the crowd, but Jesus bypassed them all. He said, "I want to go to Zacchaeus's house." He was saying, "Zacchaeus, I've been waiting for you. I knew you would be here." Jesus went to dinner with Zacchaeus and didn't berate him or tell him everything he was doing wrong. Jesus simply loved him and showed him mercy. Jesus became his friend. That day was a turning point. Zacchaeus said, "I'm going to stop being dishonest, and I'm going to start helping others by giving half my possessions to the poor. If I cheated anybody, I will pay back four times the amount." Zacchaeus changed his ways, not because he was shamed into it, but because he was loved into it. The apostle Paul says, "The goodness of God leads to repentance."

God has people in your life right now because He's counting on you, not to judge them or to find fault, but to stand in the gap. Some of the people whom we think are the furthest off course, such as

Zacchaeus and Saul, are chosen vessels. Don't give up on your child. It may have been years, but wait on them. They're going to do great things. Don't quit believing for your neighbor. They may not give you the time of day, but wait on them. God is in control.

Keep Praying

A friend of mine has a neighbor who's an older gentleman. For as long as he's known this neighbor, he's been very cynical, very negative. As a little boy, he went to church, but now he wouldn't have anything to do with God. He was bitter toward the church and all it stands for. Year after year, my friend just kept loving him, being good to him. As the neighbor grew older, my friend kept checking on him to see if there was anything he needed. One day, he found out this neighbor had been watching us on television and was going to attend one of our Nights of Hope. My friend couldn't believe it. He didn't see that coming.

You never know what God is doing behind the scenes. When you don't see anything happening, that doesn't mean God is not working. Those seeds you've been planting are still alive. The morning after the Night of Hope, my friend went to his neighbor's house. The wife had big tears in her eyes. She said, "Last night, when Joel asked people to stand to receive Christ, my husband stood up." What made it even more amazing is the man had had a stroke. He hadn't stood up on his own in years, but all by himself that night he was able to stand. He was like a different person.

I'm asking you to wait on someone. "Joel, they're off course. They're making bad decisions." So was the prodigal son, but the father waited on him. "They come from a different faith." So did the Samaritan woman at the well, but Jesus waited on her. "I've been waiting a long time, but my friend is not changing." No, your prayers are working, and things are happening that you can't see. Keep praying for them, keep encouraging them, keep showing them mercy. If you do this, I believe and

> **Your prayers are working, and things are happening that you can't see.**

declare that you're going to see your loved ones come to know the Lord. Those who are far off course—children, neighbors, friends— are being drawn in right now. As for you and your house, you will serve the Lord.

CHAPTER ELEVEN

Remember What God Said

It's not what your circumstances say, not what your feelings say, not what your mind says, not what the experts say, but what God says.

We all have promises that God has put in our hearts, things we know He's spoken to us. It may be how we're going to accomplish a dream, advance in our career, see a problem turn around, or meet the right person. At one time, we knew it was going to happen. We were praying, believing, and passionate about it. But when it's taking longer than we thought, when we've gone through disappointments, when people don't come through, when the medical report isn't improving, negative thoughts start to play louder and louder. *It's never going to work out. You're never going to be able to afford to retire. You're never going to see your family restored.* Too often we let those thoughts drown out what God has spoken to us. If you're going to stay in faith, you have to remember what God said. Go back to His promises, go back to the time when He whispered it to you in the night. Start thanking Him for what He told you. Start declaring favor, victory, and healing. You have to keep your

> It's easy to believe when things are going our way. But most of the time the promise won't come to pass without a test.

faith stirred up, keep those promises on the forefront of your mind. God is faithful. He doesn't tell you something and then not do it. The Scripture says, "All of His promises are yes and amen." It may not happen on our timetable or the way we think, but what God promised is on the way.

It's easy to believe when things are going our way. But most of the time the promise won't come to pass without a test. When you're under pressure, when you don't understand why it's taking so long and why some people didn't keep their word, you'll be tempted to live frustrated, worried, or afraid. Recognize that's a test. The enemy would love for you to forget what God promised. He'd love for you to get so caught up in what's not happening, to keep you focused on how your child isn't doing right. Right when you thought you were getting ahead, a financial setback hit. Now there's no way you think you can have a good year. No, remember what God said: "Even in a famine you will have more than enough. Whatever you touch will prosper and succeed." The economy is not your source; God is your source. You're connected to a supply line that will never run dry. But there is something always trying to steal the seed of God's Word from your heart. The enemy knows that when you keep that seed watered, when you keep thanking God for what He promised, when you keep talking like it's on the way, when you're constantly meditating on what He said, you're going to see the faithfulness of God. He's going to make things happen that you couldn't make happen.

> There is something always trying to steal the seed of God's Word from your heart.

What God Has Told You

Jesus says, "Didn't I tell you that if you believe, you will see the glory of God?" You may be facing a sickness, and you're worried and stressed out. God is saying, "Didn't I tell you that I will restore health to you? Didn't I tell you that by My stripes you are healed? Didn't I tell you that the number of your days I will fulfill?" Why don't you start thanking God for what He told you instead of letting the negative thoughts play? Many times the reason we're discouraged is that we've forgotten what God said. It's not complicated. Go back to His promises, go back to what He whispered to you in the night. Start remembering what He has spoken over you and replay that over and over. As you dwell on those promises, fear and doubt and worry have to leave, and faith will rise in your heart.

> **Why don't you start thanking God for what He told you instead of letting the negative thoughts play?**

Maybe your child is off course, running with the wrong crowd. You're frustrated, thinking they're never going to change. God is saying, "Didn't I tell you that as for you and your house, you will serve the Lord? Didn't I tell you that your children will be mighty in the land?" When you wake up in the middle of the night and are tempted to worry, turn it around. "Lord, thank You for what You say, that my children will fulfill their destiny." There's a battle taking place in our mind. The enemy comes against us with thoughts of doubt, fear, and worry. His goal is to keep your mind filled with all the negatives. He wants to keep you preoccupied with how it's not going to work out, how you can't break the addiction, or how you'll never meet the right person. He wants you to never think about what God promised you. You have to take control of your thought life. When worry comes, don't go on autopilot; don't just let it play over and over in your mind.

Stay on the offensive. Purposefully remember what God said. Thank Him that He's making a way where you don't see a way. Thank Him that He always causes you to triumph. Thank Him that what was meant for harm, He's turning to your advantage. Thank Him that

> **When worry comes, don't go on autopilot; don't just let it play over and over in your mind.**

He's taking you from glory to glory, from victory to victory.

I know a young lady who went through a relationship breakup. She'd thought this was going to be the man she would marry. She was so discouraged, so down on life and on herself. We all go through disappointments, loss, things that are not fair. If we stay focused on the hurts and keep saying, "God, why did this happen? I don't understand it," that's going to keep us weighed down and we'll miss the new things God has in store. I know it's not easy, but you have to make this shift in your thinking. Quit dwelling on the hurts and start dwelling on what God promised you. God is saying, "Didn't I tell you that I will give you beauty for those ashes? Didn't I tell you that weeping endures for a night, but joy comes in the morning? Didn't I tell you that I will pay you back double for the unfair things that have happened?" God has you in the palms of His hands. He has not brought you this far to leave you. Yes, the breakup and loss is painful, but it didn't stop your destiny. God has a new beginning. He's about to open new doors and bring new relationships. You haven't seen your best days. The enemy is fighting you because he knows there's something amazing in your future. You're on the verge of seeing blessing, favor, and influence like you've never seen. Now don't let those negative thoughts keep you where you are. Start remembering what God said.

What God Has Promised

In the Scripture, when Job was in the middle of great loss and heartache, when everything had gone wrong, it looked as though he'd seen his best days. But one of his friends said to him, "God will yet fill your mouth with laughter and your lips with shouts of joy." This was in Chapter 8, but things didn't turn around for Job until Chapter 42. I can imagine Job sitting in the ashes, discouraged, thinking about the loss of his children, his business, and his health. He was tempted to feel sorry for himself, to give up on life, but then he remembered what God promised through his friend's words. *He's going to fill my mouth with laughter.* I can hear Job saying, "Lord, thank You that I'm going to dream again, I'm going to laugh again, and I'm going to love again." Right in the middle of the difficulty, when he could have been complaining, he looked up and said, "I know that my Redeemer lives." He was saying, "I know that God is still on the throne. I know He's bigger than this adversity. I know that my latter days will be better than my former days." He kept remembering what God said, not what the circumstances said, not what his emotions said, not what the negative thoughts said. When you keep your mind on what God promised, you're going to see Him show out in your life. When that test was over, Job came out with twice what he had before.

> He kept remembering what God said, not what the circumstances said, not what his emotions said, not what the negative thoughts said.

You may have gone through loss, hurts, and disappointments, but that is not how your story ends. It may be painful now, but God sees it. He's not only going to help you get through it, but He's going to fill your mouth with laughter. There's great joy in your future. The right people are already headed your way. There are new relationships for you and favor like you've never seen. Now don't fall into the trap of complaining, living in self-pity, thinking it's all downhill from here. You're remembering the wrong things. Start remembering what God said. "There is beauty for ashes. Double is coming—double the joy, double the peace, double the resources. You're not going to just come out, you're going to come out better. You're going to come out stronger, healthier, happier, and more fulfilled." Now do like Job and keep thanking God for what He said. Keep declaring, "I know that my Redeemer lives." All through the day keep thinking, *Father, thank You that Your plans for me are for good. Thank You that You will fill my mouth with laughter again.*

When you're under pressure, what you're allowing to play in your mind is so important. Thoughts will tell you all the reasons why something's not going to work out. Sometimes people will tell you how you'll never break the addiction or you can't start a business. You have to go back to what God said, not what people say. No disrespect to them, but it's not what the experts say, not what your mind says, not how you feel, but it's what God promised. Maybe you're discouraged over how long your dream is taking, how impossible it looks. God is saying, "Didn't I tell you that what I start, I will finish? Didn't I tell you that if you delight yourself in Me, I will give you the desires of your heart?" Maybe the medical report isn't good, and now you're upset. God is saying, "Didn't I tell you that no weapon formed against you will prosper?" Perhaps people at the office are playing politics, trying to push you down. They have more influence and more seniority than you. God is saying, "Didn't I tell you that when the enemy comes in like a flood, I will raise up a barrier? Didn't I tell you that I will fight your battles

> It's not what the experts say, not what your mind says, not how you feel, but it's what God promised.

for you? Didn't I tell you that I am preparing a table before you in the presence of your enemies?" When you remember what God said, you won't be worried. You'll have peace in the midst of the storm. You'll have faith to believe for the impossible. You'll have the courage to defeat giants, the endurance to outlast the opposition, and the favor to accomplish more than you thought possible.

What God Said Overrides What You See

Early on the Sunday morning after Jesus had been crucified and had risen from the dead, three women went to the tomb to care for Jesus' body. When they arrived, they noticed something was wrong. The stone was rolled away. They looked in, and Jesus' body was gone. They were so distraught. As they sat there weeping, not knowing what to do, suddenly two men appeared to them. They were angels wearing bright robes that were so brilliant, radiating so much light, that the women could hardly look at them, and they were terrified. One of the angels said, "Why are you looking in a tomb for someone who's alive? Jesus is not here. He has risen from the dead!" I can imagine how these ladies were sitting there in awe, trying to take it all in. The angel went on to say, "Don't you remember what He told you back in Galilee, that He would be betrayed and crucified, then on the third day He would rise from the dead?" The next verse says, "Then they remembered what Jesus said, and they rushed back from the tomb to tell the disciples."

These women came to the tomb discouraged, depressed, and defeated. They went back home excited, passionate, full of faith, full of hope, and they couldn't wait to tell the other disciples. When you remember what God says, it will change your perspective. As long as you're dwelling on the negative, what didn't work out, how impossible it is, that's going to keep you discouraged. God is saying to you what the angel said to them, "Don't you remember what I told you? Don't you remember that I said you will lend and not borrow? Don't you remember

> **When you remember what God says, it will change your perspective.**

I said that My mercy is bigger than your mistakes?" God has you reading this for one reason, so you'll remember what He's promised you. You need to go back to what God has spoken to you, go back to the dream He gave you in the night, go back to the promise that He whispered in your spirit. You have to stir it up. Get your passion back. Get your hopes up. Start talking like it's on the way. Start thanking God that it's coming.

The Scripture says these ladies were perplexed, overwhelmed, confused. Their world had been turned upside-down. Under all the pressure, with all the stress and grief of losing their friend, they forgot what Jesus had told them. What's interesting is that He had told them all of this was going to happen just a few days before, not twenty years earlier. It would make sense if they'd forgotten because it had been a long time. But when they came under the pressure, when they felt over-whelmed, they forgot what He'd said. That's the time you have to be on guard. When life is stressful, when you have a

> **When life is stressful, when you have a setback in your finances, or when you're struggling with depression, don't let those negative thoughts drown out what God promised.**

setback in your finances, or when you're struggling with depression, don't let those negative thoughts drown out what God promised.

Maybe you're under pressure now. Perhaps circumstances in your life have you feeling anxious and worried, thinking, *What's going to happen with my finances? What about my children?* Maybe you've felt that you've had to put your life on hold. It's easy to forget what God promised. Like that angel, I'm saying to remember what God told you. You may feel alone, but He said, "I'll never leave you. I'll stick closer than a brother." Perhaps your business has slowed down, and you don't know how you're going to make ends meet. He said, "I'll make streams in the desert. I'll supply your needs according to My riches." The anxiety, the depression, or the addiction may seem permanent. He said, "The enemies you see today you will see no more. Greater is He who is in you than what's trying to stop you. Whom the Son sets free is unquestionably free."

Are you remembering what He said? Or have you let the circumstances, the trouble, and the stress cause you to dwell on the negative, to think about how it's not going to work out? When we're under pressure, the mistake we often make is to go by what we see instead of by what God said. "Well, Joel, look at this medical report. Look at my finances. Look at how big these obstacles are." As long as you go by what you see, you're going to be worried and stressed. You have to start going by what God said. Here's the good news: What He said will override what you see.

> As long as you go by what you see, you're going to be worried and stressed.

When my father passed and I stepped up to pastor the church, what I saw when I looked in the mirror was someone who was inexperienced, intimidated, and unqualified. Thoughts told me that nobody would listen to me, that I was going to get up there and fail. I was tempted to live worried and shrink back, but I did what I'm asking you to do. I didn't go by what I saw; I went by what God said. I felt weak, but I remembered that God said, "I am strong in the Lord." I didn't think I could do it, but I remembered that God said, "I can do all things through Christ." I had some people who didn't want me to succeed, some critics who had large followings and seemed to want to discredit me, to hold me down, but I remembered that God said, "Promotion doesn't come from people; it comes from the Lord." People don't determine your destiny. They cannot stop the calling on your life. They may look bigger, more powerful, and more influential. Don't go by what you see; go by what God says. He says, "You're a giant killer. You're more than a conqueror. The trap the enemies set for you, they will fall in themselves."

Focus on What God Said

In Matthew 14, after Jesus fed a crowd of thousands with five loaves and two fish, He told the disciples to get in the boat and cross over to the other side of the lake. He said He would send the crowd home. The disciples started rowing that way, and everything was going fine until the winds picked up and the waves got rough. For hours they were struggling to make it. At three o'clock in the morning, they looked through the darkness and saw this figure coming toward them, walking on the water. They thought it was a ghost and were so afraid that the Scripture says, "They screamed in terror." They had never seen anything like this. Jesus told them, "Take courage. I am here." Peter was not only astonished, he was inspired. He said, "Lord, if it's really You, tell me to come to You, walking on the water." Jesus said, "Yes, come." Peter climbed over the side of the boat and stepped into the water but his feet didn't go down. He started walking on top of the water, defying the odds. I can imagine how amazed he was, how in awe. He took step after step, looking at Jesus, marveling at what was happening. But then he began to look around at the waves, at how strong the wind was, at how the boat was rocking, and how he was out in the middle of the water. Suddenly he began to sink. He cried out, "Lord, please save me!" Jesus reached down and helped him back into the boat.

As long as Peter was focused on what Jesus said—"Walk on the water. Come here with Me"—he was fine. But when he started focusing on what he saw—the winds, the waves—he began to doubt, to be afraid and think, *I can't do this.* It's the same principle in life. If you stay focused on what you see, you can get talked out of your dreams. If you're focused on how big the obstacles are, how the medical report is not good, or how you'll never get out of debt, you'll be limited. You have to stay focused on what God said. When you focus on what He promised, you'll walk on water. You'll go places you couldn't go on your own. You'll overcome obstacles that are much bigger. The winds and the waves are a test. Are you going to get distracted and start focusing on the negative? *This problem is too big. This addiction seems permanent. I don't have the finances to go to college. I'll never get out of this neighborhood.* That's going to cause you to sink. You have to change your focus from what you see to what God said. You have to walk by faith and not by sight.

> When you focus on what He promised, you'll walk on water. You'll go places you couldn't go on your own.

What you're up against may seem impossible, but God created you to walk on water. He created you to defy the odds. He created you to go further than people say you can go. He created you to defeat giants. He created you to beat the cancer. He created you to acquire Compaq Centers. Yes, it seems unlikely. Yes, you may not feel that you have the talent. Yes, you may be afraid. That's okay. The key is to not focus on what you see; focus on what God said. That's what's going to fuel your faith. That's when you're going to see far-and-beyond favor that catapults you ahead.

You Can't Go By What You See

God put a desire in the heart of Nehemiah to rebuild the broken-down walls of Jerusalem. But Nehemiah wasn't a builder. He was a cupbearer to the king of Persia, living a thousand miles away from Jerusalem. He didn't have any resources, any staff, or any influence. But God never asks you to do something and then doesn't give you the ability to do it. God was saying to Nehemiah, "You're going to walk on water, you're going to do something over your head, something that you're not qualified for, something where you don't have the connections or the experience." Nehemiah could have looked at the circumstances and thought, *God, You have the wrong person. I'll never accomplish this dream.* But Nehemiah understood this principle. He didn't go by what he saw; he went by what God said.

When you step out in faith, God will open doors that no person can shut. He'll bring the right people. He'll make things happen that you couldn't make happen. God gave Nehemiah favor with the Persian king. The king not only let him have the time off, which was unprecedented, but he gave Nehemiah a letter requiring people to give him the materials and resources he needed. It should have taken years, but Nehemiah rebuilt the walls in just fifty-two days. God has some things in your future where you're going to walk on water. You're going to accomplish what seems impossible. You're going to overcome what looks insurmountable. Now do your part and don't focus on the winds, the waves, the impossibilities. That's going to talk you out of it. Focus on what God said. Let His promises play in your mind over and over. Thank God every day for the dream that He put

> **Dare to believe that the secret things He whispered to you in the night are on the way.**

in your heart. Dare to believe that the secret things He whispered to you in the night are on the way.

A friend of mine knew an older gentleman who was a fighter pilot in World War II. He not only flew missions but he was a flight trainer of young men, many of them only eighteen years old. Before he took them up in the air, they spent hours going over the instruments, learning what they did, what caused the plane to function. He stressed the importance of always flying the plane by the instruments, not by what they saw. They spent months and months on the ground in flight simulators, flying planes strictly by the instruments. After one young pilot completed the program, the trainer took him up in the air. The new pilot was doing great, everything was running smoothly, just like his training. But a few minutes later, a huge thunderstorm suddenly arose. The plane started bouncing around as it entered the dark clouds. It got to the point where they couldn't see anything. Instead of going by his instruments and following his training, the young pilot panicked and looked at all the clouds and the rain and felt the plane shaking. He became disoriented and confused. He couldn't tell if he was gaining or losing altitude. He kept straining to see out the window to try to get a visual sign as to which direction to go. Finally, the flight instructor took a blanket that was used to cover the windshield when the plane was stored, and he clipped it in place. Now the young pilot couldn't see anything. He had no choice except to go by the instruments. In a few minutes, they came out of the storm and eventually landed the plane safely.

Like this young pilot, sometimes we know what God promised us; we have the instruments. We do fine in our training on the ground. We quote the Scripture and believe, but when the storm of trouble hits, we start looking at the problems and obstacles. It's bumpy, and we don't see a way. Too often, we panic and live worried, but you have to come back to the instruments. You can't go by what you see or you'll get discouraged. You may not see anything except dark clouds.

Everywhere you look, there's no visibility. There's no sign of how it's going to work out. Go back to your instruments. Remember what God promised you. There's not a storm you're facing that's a surprise to God. There's not a problem you're in that He can't get you out of. But when you're under pressure, when life gets stressful, it's easy to focus on the wrong things.

Are you looking out the window, focused on the storm, or are you focused on what God promised you? He's spoken dreams to your heart. He's whispered things to you in the night. The enemy has tried to drown them out with negative thoughts and negative circumstances, but they are still alive. What God started, He's going to finish. Now do your part and remember what He said. Keep declaring what He promised. Keep thanking Him for it. If you do this, I believe and declare that you're going to walk on water like Peter did. You're going to defy the odds like Nehemiah did and accomplish dreams bigger than you thought. Like the pilot, you're going to come through every storm safely and soar to new heights.

> Are you looking out the window, focused on the storm, or are you focused on what God promised you?

CHAPTER TWELVE

God Has the Final Say

The sovereign God, the God who reigns, has the last word and will finish what He started in your life.

We all have situations that look permanent, like they're never going to work out. It's easy to get discouraged and think it's not meant to be. The enemy will do everything he can to convince you that it's over. The medical report looks too bad. The financial advisor says there's no way you can pay off your debt. The naysayers keep telling you that the economy is going into a recession that will take your business down. But none of them are on the throne. God is on the throne, and it's not over until He says it's over. God being for you is more than the world being against you. He won't allow you to get in a problem that He can't get you out of.

In Daniel 3, God wouldn't have let the three Hebrew teenagers be thrown into a fiery furnace if He didn't know the fire wasn't going to harm them. King Nebuchadnezzar thought he was in control. He thought he had the final say. He was certain the fire would finish them off, just as it always had others. But this time he wasn't dealing with ordinary people; he was dealing with children of the Most High God. They came out of the furnace without even the smell of smoke. There's something about you that makes you unstoppable. You have an advantage. The Creator of the universe not only breathed life into you, but He put a hedge of protection around you. Nothing can touch you without His permission. You're not at the mercy of bad breaks, accidents, sicknesses, or people who are against you. None of that can stop your destiny.

> The Creator of the universe not only breathed life into you, but He put a hedge of protection around you. Nothing can touch you without His permission.

Some people think, *If I can just get my supervisor to like me, maybe I'll get the promotion.* No, you don't have to play up to people. When you go to work, be your best and let your talent shine. When it's time to be promoted, all the forces of darkness cannot hold you back. You may say, "My boss doesn't like me." Your boss doesn't have the final say. He's a pawn in the hand of God. You're not doing life by yourself. God is behind the scenes pulling strings, orchestrating things in your favor. At the right time, God will either cause that boss to promote you or move them out of the way. They can't stop your purpose. When you know God has the final say, you don't live frustrated, trying to manipulate people. You stay in peace, knowing that nothing can stop God's plan.

What He Says Goes

When the prophet Samuel came to Jesse's house to pick out one of his sons as the next king of Israel, Jesse lined up seven of his sons and said, "All right, Samuel, take your pick." Jesse didn't bother to bring his youngest son, David, in from the shepherds' fields. He had already ruled David out, thinking, *He's too small, too young, not talented. He's not king material.* This would have been a problem if people have the final say. If people determine our destiny, we would never have heard about David. But while it may be hurtful when people leave you out, it

> **What God has for you is not going to go to anyone else.**

doesn't stop your purpose. Samuel said, "Jesse, I don't see the king in these seven sons. Do you have any other sons?" This shows us that what God has for you is not going to go to anyone else. When people try to manipulate things, discredit you, or leave you out, don't worry. God is on the throne. He's pulling the strings. He knew who wasn't going to like you, who was going to try to push you down. You don't have to try to get even or straighten people out. Stay in peace, keep doing the right thing, and the promotion will come to you.

Jesse sent word for David to come into the house. When Samuel saw him, he said, "There's the next king of Israel." God doesn't choose like we choose. We look on the outside—a person's size, looks, talent, and personality. God looks at the heart. People may have counted you out, but don't worry. God has already counted you in. He overrides what people say. He overrides the injustice. "Joel, I'm in an unfair situation, but nothing is changing." It's not over yet. That's not how your story ends. Your time is coming. Like with David, you're going to be called into the house. God hasn't forgotten about you. What He promised is still on the way. Bad breaks didn't stop it. People didn't cancel it. Delays don't mean it's not going to happen. What God started, He's going to finish. He has the final say.

Now stay in faith. Don't go around talking about how it's not going to happen. "This illness is going to be the end of me. I never get any good breaks. I'll never accomplish my dreams." When you say that, you're putting your circumstances on the throne. You're saying, in effect, that circumstances have the final say, that other people control your destiny. You need to take the problem off the throne and put God back on the throne. God is sovereign over your circumstances. That means God reigns over everything you face. He doesn't just rule the universe. He reigns over sicknesses, over your finances, and over your children.

The apostle Peter says, "Jesus has the last word on everything and everyone, from angels to armies. He's standing right alongside God, and what He says goes." You may be dealing with a sickness, and the medical report says you're not going to make it. That's one word, but God has the last word. The sovereign God, the God who reigns, says, "I'm restoring health to you." Keep Him on the throne. When thoughts tell you that you're never going to get well, just say, "No thanks. I know a secret. My God has the final say. Sickness may have a say, depression may have a say, injustice may have a say, but I have news for them. What they say is subject to the God who created me. What they say is overruled by the Most High God. He has the final word on everything and everyone."

> **"Jesus has the last word on everything and everyone, from angels to armies. He's standing right alongside God, and what He says goes."**

What He Promises Will Happen

God promised Abraham that he and his wife, Sarah, were going to have a baby, but they were way too old. Sarah had gone through the change of life. There was no way in the natural that they could have a child. Sometimes God will put things in your heart that don't make sense to your mind. It's easy to dismiss it and think it could never happen. But the Scripture says, "Abraham considered not the weakness of his own body or the deadness of Sarah's womb." He didn't deny that her womb was dead. He didn't ignore the facts. He just didn't dwell on it. He didn't go around talking about how impossible it was and how it could never happen. He knew that God wouldn't have given him the promise if He wasn't going to bring it to pass. If you're going to stay in faith, you have to do as Abraham did and not consider what looks dead. Don't dwell on what seems impossible. Are you spending more time thinking about the problem or the promise? Are you talking more about how big the challenge is or about how big your God is?

> **Do as Abraham did and not consider what looks dead. Don't dwell on what seems impossible.**

If Sarah had gone in for a checkup, the doctor would have said, "Sorry, but you're too old to have a child. Your womb is no longer fertile. You waited too long, and it's not possible." No doctor would have given her a chance of getting pregnant. Don't let people talk you out of what God put in your heart. Don't let experts convince you that it's not going to happen. Remember that experts built the *Titanic* and it sank; amateurs built the ark and it floated. Sometimes the experts can be wrong. They don't know what God has put in you. They can't see the seeds of greatness inside. On your own, what they're saying may be true, but you have the most powerful force in the universe breathing in your direction.

Don't Get Talked Out of It

God has the final say over your dreams. People may have discouraged you, but what He promised is on the way. He has the final say over your health. It may not have happened yet, but healing is coming. He has the final say over your children. He knows how to get the attention of a child who's off course. He says, "As for you and your house, you will serve the Lord." It would be one thing if God had a say—that would be encouraging—but God has the last word. He overrides what's trying to stop you. The opposition you face, the people who are against you, have a say. They may set you back, but really they're setting you up. The more they pull you back, the further God is going to shoot you. He has the final say.

When Abraham was a hundred years old and Sarah was ninety, twenty-five years after the promise, they came into the final word. Sarah gave birth to a son. God overrode the laws of nature, overrode what the experts said, and overrode the mistakes they had made. If Abraham were here today, he would tell you not to let the circumstances talk you out of what God put in your heart. It may look dead, it may seem too late, and all the experts may tell you it's impossible, but I can tell you firsthand, "God has the final say."

> God overrode the laws of nature, overrode what the experts said, and overrode the mistakes they had made.

Think about Joseph in the Old Testament. His brothers had a say—they were jealous, betrayed him, and sold him into slavery in Egypt. Potiphar, the man he worked for, had a say—he had Joseph put in prison when his wife lied about him. Joseph was good to a fellow prisoner, interpreted another prisoner's dream and encouraged him. But when the prisoner was released, he forgot all about Joseph. There were a lot of negative voices, negative circumstances, in Joseph's life. He could have been bitter, but he understood that God has the final say. After all the disappointments and bad breaks, Joseph was suddenly called out of the prison and made the prime minister of Egypt. When God has the final say, it will make up for all the injustice, all the delays. You may be falling behind, but you're not losing time. One touch of God's favor will put you fifty years down the road—not in age, but in influence, in position, in opportunity.

I believe that you are about to see God step in and override what's been hindering you like He did for Joseph. You've been doing the right thing, honoring God, being good to people. Now God is about

> **God is about to show out. You're about to see the final say in your health, in your career, in your finances.**

to show out. You're about to see the final say in your health, in your career, in your finances. That struggle looked permanent. It looks like you will never get ahead, but God is about to override the lack, the limitations, or the people who have held you back. He's about to release you into new levels of increase and abundance. The final word is: "You will lend and not borrow. You are above and not beneath." Maybe you were raised in dysfunction, with addictions, with depression. The final word is coming. God is about to break those yokes that have pulled you down so you can step up to who you were created to be. The final word is freedom, wholeness, abundance, and victory.

What You've Given Up On

In the Scripture, Mary and Martha and their brother Lazarus were close friends with Jesus. Lazarus became very sick while Jesus was in another city. Martha sent word asking Jesus to come pray for their brother. They had seen Jesus heal people, open the eyes of the blind, and make the crippled walk. They knew He had turned water into wine and could do miracles. Jesus received the news that Lazarus was sick, but he stayed in that city. A day went by, two days, three days. Then their worst nightmare came true. Lazarus died. They were

> **Has it ever seemed like God showed up too late for you?**

so upset. Four days later, Jesus finally showed up. Has it ever seemed like God showed up too late for you? You prayed, you stood in faith, but the medical report wasn't good, and the problem didn't turn around, the business didn't make it. When Martha saw Jesus, she was so upset. She said, "Jesus, if You had been here sooner, my brother would not have died." Martha could have walked away and lived bitter, and that would be the end of the story. But she said, "I know even now, whatever You ask, God will do it for You." She was saying, "This looks bad. It seems impossible. But I know that You have the final say."

Jesus said to them, "Take Me to where you buried Lazarus. Take Me to the tomb." He was saying, "Take Me to the place where you quit believing. Take Me to the place where you gave up on your dream, where you decided you'd never get well or you wouldn't meet the right person." Unless you go back to that place and stir up your faith, start thanking God that He has the final say, that will limit what God can do. They went to the tomb, and Jesus told them to roll away the stone. Martha said, "Lord, he's been dead four days. He's going to stink." The stone represents what you've given up on. You think it's been too long, it didn't happen in time. So you put the stone over the promise, you put the stone over the dream. You have to do your part and roll that stone away. You have to start believing again. Get your passion back.

They rolled away the stone, but Jesus didn't go in and lay hands on Lazarus like He did with the blind man and many others who were healed. This time He spoke, saying, "Lazarus, come forth!" All of a sudden Lazarus woke up. He came out of the tomb on a word from the Lord. Jesus may not be here in person, but we have what Lazarus had. You can come out on a word from God. He says, "You will live and not die." Let that take root, and you can come out on that word. "Whatever you touch will prosper and succeed." There's a word to come out on. "Whom the Son sets free is free indeed." There's a word to break bondages. What God says in the Scripture is the final word.

> **What God says in the Scripture is the final word.**

It's significant that Jesus waited four days to go pray for Lazarus. He knew Lazarus was sick. He could have gone the first day and healed him, and it would have saved a lot of trouble. Or He could have gone at least by the second day and not made them go through so much. But there's always a reason for a delay. We may not understand it, but God knows what He's doing. If Martha had stayed negative and sour, it could have stopped the miracle. This is where many people miss it. While you're waiting for

Will you stay in faith when God is silent?

a situation to turn around, waiting for your circumstances to improve, waiting for a child to get on the right course, that's a test you have to pass. Will you stay in faith when God is silent? Will you wait with a good attitude, thanking God that He has the final say, when nothing is changing? How you wait will determine whether or not your situation changes.

In those days, the Sadducees were one of the religious groups that were against Jesus. They believed that the spirit left the body three days after a person died. It's not a coincidence that Jesus waited until the fourth day to show up. He did this so that when He raised Lazarus, there wouldn't be any doubt about it. Sometimes God will wait on purpose not only so you will know it is His favor, but so will your critics, friends, relatives, and coworkers. They won't be able to deny the goodness of God in your life.

He Has Planned Your Days

I talked to a lady whose son was diagnosed with muscular dystrophy at six years old. He got to the point where he couldn't walk. When he was twelve, he went in for surgery on his feet and heels. It was a routine procedure, but something went wrong. He ended up in ICU on a ventilator, unable to breathe on his own. His heart, lungs, and kidneys started shutting down, then he had to go on dialysis. The doctors told his mother that it didn't look as though he was going to make it. She kept praying and believing, but everything went downhill. It got to the point where they had to put him on a machine to bypass his heart and lungs. Basically, he was on life support, just waiting to pass. They went to get the papers for the mother to sign. While she was waiting, the doctor came rushing in and said, "Hold on! You don't need to sign. There's been a change." The doctors couldn't explain it, but his heart suddenly started working, his blood pressure stabilized, and his lungs began to function. They couldn't understand how he was dying one moment and the next moment he was coming back to life.

God has the final say. If it's not your time to go, you're not going to go. The Scripture says, "The number of your days, God will fulfill." You don't have to do it; God is going to fulfill it. Nothing can snatch you out of His hands. A sickness cannot take you before the time God has planned for you. "Well, Joel, my loved one didn't make it." Then their time was up. They fulfilled the days God had planned for them. They didn't go to Heaven unannounced. They didn't show up and hear God say, "Wow! I didn't see you coming." God was the one bidding them to come. He was the One welcoming them into His arms. To say that illness took your loved one before their time is to say the sickness is bigger than our God.

> To say that illness took your loved one before their time is to say the sickness is bigger than our God.

We may not understand it, and we may not like it, but you can rest assured God has the final say. He planned your days before you were born, and He promised He will fulfill the number of your days.

That young man totally recovered. He's twenty-five years old now. He can walk, he's no longer on dialysis, his heart and his lungs are fine. He's fulfilling his purpose. You may have a situation like this mother faced that doesn't look like it will ever turn around—a dream that seems impossible, an addiction that looks permanent. I believe you're going to hear what she heard: "There's been a sudden change. Something we can't explain has taken place." You thought you had reached your limits, gone as far as you can, when you're promoted suddenly, the company wants you to run your department. After so many years, you thought you'd always struggle with an addiction, but get ready: A sudden change is coming. Forces of darkness are being broken. Any area of your life where you're not living in victory is not permanent; it's temporary. The final say is coming.

It's Not Over Until God Says So

My brother-in-law, Don, graduated from Texas A&M University and is a huge Aggie football fan. In 2018, he was watching a big game with one of their main rivals. The lead was going back and forth, and it came down to the final possession...just a few seconds left. The Aggies needed to score to tie the game, but the quarterback threw an interception and the other team got the ball. They poured Gatorade on their coach, started celebrating, running out on the field, and the opposing fans went wild. Don was so upset that he not only turned the television off, he deleted the recording from his DVR. He didn't even want that game in his files. Half an hour later, a friend texted him saying, "This game is unbelievable!" Don thought his friend must have recorded it and was watching what he'd already seen, but then he looked on Twitter and saw a stream of other comments. As it turned out, before the Aggie quarterback threw the interception, his knee was down. That meant the play was over. The referees reviewed it and gave the ball back to the Aggies. They went on to score and tie the game. The game went into overtime, then a second overtime, a third overtime, and in the seventh overtime, the Aggies won the game. It was one of the greatest games in college history.

Sometimes in life we do like Don and turn the game off too soon. We think we'll never get well, never meet the right person, or never accomplish a dream. We tried, and it didn't work out. It feels as though the opposition has won; now they're celebrating and pouring Gatorade on the coach. Can I tell you that it's not over until God says it's over? You better go back and look again. Your story doesn't end in defeat; it ends in victory. Along the way, there may be some temporary setbacks, times when it looks as though it's not possible, it's too late, but God has ways you never thought of. Get your passion back and start believing again. The game is still on.

> **Your story doesn't end in defeat; it ends in victory.**

This is what happened over two thousand years ago. Satan and all the forces of darkness were celebrating. They had already shot the confetti, poured the Gatorade, and started their victory party. They had finally defeated Jesus, watched Him be nailed to the cross and take His last breath. What they didn't realize was that Jesus had prophesied not only His death but His resurrection. They got the first part of the message, but they didn't get the final word. Jesus said, "Destroy this temple, and I will raise it again in three days." Not having a tomb of His own, Jesus was buried in a tomb owned by Joseph of Arimathea. Jesus was saying, in effect, "I don't need to buy it. I'm only going to use Joseph's tomb for three days." Satan had selective hearing. While they were all partying, having their big celebration, Jesus showed up, took away the keys of death and hell, and said, "I am He that lives. I was dead but I am alive forevermore."

Today, the enemy may be celebrating over you, thinking that you're done. He thinks he's convinced you that you've seen your best days, that you'll always be depressed, always be lonely, always be addicted. You need to let him know, "You didn't hear the final word. I might have fallen, but I will arise. I may be fighting an illness, but healing is coming. This difficulty in my marriage is not permanent; restoration is on the way. This setback in my finances is not how my story ends; abundance is in my future." The final word says your latter days will be better than your former days. The final word says what God started in your life, He will finish. The final word says you will live and not die.

Now get in agreement with God. Go back to those places where you quit believing and stir up your faith. Who told you it was over? That wasn't the final word. Like with Lazarus, it may have been dead, but I believe and declare that it's coming back to life. You're about to see God show out. There's a sudden change coming— sudden healing, sudden opportunities, sudden promotion, sudden breakthroughs. What you thought was permanent is about to change in your favor. God is going to not just bring promises to pass, not just turn problems around, but it's going to turn out better than you ever imagined.

> **Who told you it was over? That wasn't the final word.**

START PRAYING BOLD TODAY

It's exciting to know that when you release your faith in uncommon ways, you'll see God do uncommon things. The apostle John wrote: "This is the confidence we have in approaching God: that if we ask anything according to His will, He hears us. And if we know that He hears us—whatever we ask—we know that we have what we asked of Him." If you're asking according to God's will, you can be confident that yes is the answer.

Whether you've been waiting for an answer to a difficult situation for a long time, or you're facing an obstacle that feels overwhelming, or you need strength to make it through a dry season, the prayers that follow will build your faith and help you pray prayers that move the hands of God. There are prayers you can pray for peace and comfort, for your family and health, for your dreams and goals. As you make these prayers your own, you'll pray with confidence, and that's when you'll see the Creator of the universe go to work. Praying bold will put you on the right path. You'll enter new seasons in your prayer life and turn challenges to victories, heartache to hope, frustration to newfound favor.

These prayers are based upon promises in God's Word, which is where we discover His will. You don't have to beg, you don't have to wonder, and you don't have to keep asking. Just believe and receive His promises in your spirit and accept His yes by faith. Then take the next step and keep thanking Him that you've received it, and watch what God will do.

30 BOLD PRAYERS

For Freedom from Regrets and Guilt

Father, thank You that You are a merciful God, the One who blots out my wrongs and remembers my sins no more. Thank You that when Jesus declared "It is finished" on the cross, it meant He had fully paid the incredible price for my past mistakes, that He released me from the guilt and shame, and broke the chains of regret over things I've done. I declare that I am forgiven and redeemed and free from condemnation. I declare "Shame off me!" to whatever tries to make me feel unworthy. When the accusing voices start in, I will simply turn them off. Help me to let go of the past, to walk in the joy of my salvation, and to believe that Your mercies are new every morning. In Jesus' name, Amen.

> *"Oh, what joy for those whose disobedience is forgiven, whose sins are put out of sight. Yes, what joy for those whose record the LORD has cleared of sin."*
>
> Romans 4:7–8 NLT

For Fresh Vision

Father, thank You that You are the God who spoke worlds into existence, the God who is always doing something new, and Your plans for my life are always good. Thank You that You are breathing fresh vision and strength into me, new seasons, new dreams, new relationships, new beginnings. I believe that even now You are working in ways I don't yet see and You're about to do a new thing. Help me to clear out all the negative, limited thinking, and open my eyes to the increase and the great things You want to bring into my life. I am enlarging my vision and making room for abundance and blessings. I declare that nothing is going to keep me from what You have in store. In Jesus' name, Amen.

> *"Forget about what's happened; don't keep going over old history. Be alert, be present. I'm about to do something brand-new. It's bursting out! Don't you see it?"*
> Isaiah 43:18–19 MSG

For Healing and Wholeness

Father, thank You that You are Jehovah Rapha, the Lord my healer and miracle worker. Thank You that You say that it is Your will to heal all diseases and restore health back to me. Your Word says that by Jesus' stripes I am healed and that Your desire is for me to have a long, healthy life that is truly satisfying. I declare that sickness has no right to my body, and I come boldly to receive all the blessings and healing power of Jesus. Open my eyes to see all that He has done for me and to receive the wholeness He purchased for me on the cross. I declare that healing, wholeness, strength, and vitality are flowing into me right now and that my youth is being renewed like an eagle's. In Jesus' name, Amen.

> *"For I will restore health to you, and your wounds I will heal, declares the LORD."*
>
> Jeremiah 30:17 ESV

For Joy

Father, thank You that I can come boldly into Your presence, where there is fullness of joy right now, because Jesus has made a way for me. Thank You that You are my God, my exceeding joy, and You fill me with inexpressible joy. No matter what I face today, I receive Your joy as my strength, like an abundant stream that comes from within and runs deeper than my emotional ups and downs. I refuse to allow people and circumstances to get me upset and steal my joy. I've made up my mind that I'm going to rejoice in You and be glad. Help me to put a smile on my face and spread joy everywhere I go. In Jesus' name, Amen.

> *Though you have not seen him, you love him; and even though you do not see him now, you believe in him and are filled with an inexpressible and glorious joy.*
>
> 1 Peter 1:8 NIV

For Letting Go

Thank You that there is no other God like You, the Most High God. Thank You that You are always going ahead in my life, lining up the next level, and You're not in the past. Right now I am letting go of any lingering negative baggage that comes from carrying past offenses, mistakes, guilt, and blame. I choose to let go of any anger, hurt, and bitterness and to forgive others from past offenses. Help me to treat yesterday's discouragements, disappointments, guilt, fears, and doubts as dead and buried once and for all and leave the past as the past. I will become an expert at letting go of the old, looking straight ahead, and focusing my energy on pressing forward into the good things You have in store for me. In Jesus' name, Amen.

I am bringing all my energies to bear on this one thing:
Forgetting the past and looking forward to what lies ahead.
Philippians 3:13 TLB

For Overcoming Anxiety and Worry

Father, thank You that You are the Good Shepherd who leads me to lie down beside restful waters. Thank You for being on the throne of my life and that my health, my finances, my family, and my circumstances are all in the palms of Your hands. I have Your promise that You will work out Your plans for my life, for Your faithful love endures forever. I choose to let go of the worrisome thoughts that trap me in anxiety, fear, and discouragement, and I come to You with my needs, which are no match for You. I receive Your supernatural peace and rest, knowing that You will provide everything I need for every season I am in. In Jesus' name, Amen.

> *Do not be anxious about anything, but in every situation, by prayer and petition, with thanksgiving, present your requests to God. And the peace of God, which transcends all understanding, will guard your hearts and your minds in Christ Jesus.*
>
> Philippians 4:6–7 NIV

For Victory in the Battle

Father, thank You that You are the great God, the King of kings, the Mighty Warrior who saves. Yours is the greatness, the power, the glory, the victory, and the majesty. Thank You for the promise of an overwhelming victory through Jesus' triumph over the grave and all the forces of darkness. Your Word says that You are fighting my battles and making me more than a conqueror, a victor and never a victim of circumstances. I declare that Your power to strengthen me in times of difficulty is greater than the greatest force that can ever come against me. I'm going to stay in peace knowing that no obstacle that stands in my way can stop Your plan. I believe that You will do exceedingly abundantly above all that I ask or think. In Jesus' name, Amen.

> *Yet in all these things we are more than conquerors and*
> *gain an overwhelming victory through Him who loved us.*
>
> Romans 8:37 AMP

For Victory over Fear

Father, thank You that You are my light and my salvation, the stronghold of my life, the Guardian of my soul. Of whom or what shall I be afraid? Thank You that no matter what happens in my life, I have Your promise that You are with me and always lead me to triumph through Jesus. I come into Your presence and declare that Your perfect love casts out my fear. I declare that no weapon formed against me shall prosper. I boldly confess that with Your power, I have strength to do all things. I choose to close the door on fear by guarding what I say, what I listen to, and what I dwell on. I will live from a place of peace, knowing I am safe in the palms of Your hands. I will not be afraid. I will believe. In Jesus' name, Amen.

> *But overhearing what they said, Jesus said to the ruler of the synagogue, "Do not fear, only believe."*
>
> Mark 5:36 ESV

For Your Family

Father, thank You that You are the Creator of the universe as well as my family and that every good gift and every perfect gift that we enjoy comes down to us from You, the Father of lights. Thank You for loving my family with an everlasting love. You are our refuge, our fortress, our God, and it's in You we trust. Help me to treasure my loved ones as marvelous gifts, to speak words of life, faith, and encouragement to them, and to stir up their dreams and give them permission to succeed. Use me to show them how deep Your love is for them. May joy and laughter and peace and understanding fill our times together and may You make our hearts to be one. I believe that You are taking my family to the next level. In Jesus' name, Amen.

> *"As for me and my family, we will serve the LORD."*
>
> Joshua 24:15 NLT

For Your Finances

Father, thank You that You are Jehovah Jireh, the Lord my provider. Thank You for Your promise to supply all my needs according to Your glorious riches in Christ Jesus. Thank You that You say that even in famine, the righteous will have more than enough. I believe You are my source, not the economy or my job, and that I am connected to a supply line that will never run dry. Give me wisdom about how to handle my finances and to keep me from making foolish decisions. I believe that You delight in prospering me and that I can use my finances as a tool for good. I believe for overflow to bless others. I declare favor is on my finances and set my trust wholly in You. In Jesus' name, Amen.

> *"You shall remember the LORD your God, for it is he who gives you power to get wealth."*
>
> Deuteronomy 8:18 ESV

In Times of Disappointment

Father, thank You that You are the God who goes before me and levels the mountains of disappointment and discouragement. Thank You that You give beauty for ashes, the oil of joy for mourning, the garment of praise for the spirit of heaviness. When doors close, hurts and setbacks come, someone walks away, or plans fail, help me to remember that You are still on the throne and my future is set in Your hands. I believe that You can turn what's unfair into a positive, the bitter into sweet, the no into a yes, the question mark into an exclamation point, the defeat into victory. You promise that my hope and expectancy in You will never be disappointed, that You are directing my steps through the disappointments, and that my path will get brighter and brighter. I declare that I will keep being my best, serving, giving, and loving right where I am. In Jesus' name, Amen.

> *"The LORD himself goes before you and will be with you; he*
> *will never leave you nor forsake you. Do not be afraid; do*
> *not be discouraged."*
>
> Deuteronomy 31:8 NIV

In Times of Doubt

Father, thank You that You are love, that You love me just as I am, and You want the real me to come to You. Thank You that You never fault me for being honest about my doubts, my struggles, my weaknesses, or my fears. When doubts whisper in my mind, when the enemy tries to get me to question what You have said in Your Word, help me to remember that no word from You has ever failed, and that's reason enough to never waver in believing Your promises. Today, I resist the enemy and his lies, firm in my faith, and I put the clutter of doubts far from me. I choose to tune out the voice of doubt and only listen to and obey the voice of faith. I believe that Your words and promises to me will be fulfilled. Increase my faith to believe big, dream big, pray big, and think big. In Jesus' name, Amen.

The father cried, "Then I believe. Help me with my doubts!"
Mark 9:24 MSG

In Tough Times

Father, thank You that You are my fortress and my refuge in the tough times, and that You surround me with a shield of favor at all times. Thank You that You hear every prayer that I whisper in the dark and through the seasons of struggle and pressure, seasons of silence, seasons of patiently waiting, seasons of opposition and pain. Your Word says that You refine my life with fire and use every test of my faith to prepare me to overcome and persevere for the greater that is coming—greater honor, joy, opportunities, and victory. I am absolutely confident as I keep moving forward in faith that You will make a way through the difficulties and amaze me with what You have planned. I declare that I am coming out better off than I was before. In Jesus' name, Amen.

These troubles and sufferings of ours are, after all, quite small and won't last very long. Yet this short time of distress will result in God's richest blessing upon us forever and ever!
2 Corinthians 4:17 TLB

To Believe for the Impossible

Father, thank You that there is no other God like You, so majestic in holiness, awesome in glory, working wonders through Your mighty power to accomplish infinitely more than I can ask or think. Thank You that one touch of Your favor can part Red Seas, close the mouths of lions, open the eyes of the blind, and raise the dead. I am limited, but You have an unlimited supply of everything I need in this life. I believe that You take the loaves and the fishes in my life, my dreams and goals, and multiply them when I put them in Your hands. When You put a promise in my heart that seems impossible, that looks too big, I want to always respond with three simple words: "Lord, I believe." You specialize in doing the impossible, and You have the final word. My eyes are on You to do what only You can do. In Jesus' name, Amen.

> *Jesus looked at them intently and said, "Humanly speaking, it is impossible. But not with God. Everything is possible with God."*
>
> Mark 10:27 NLT

To Break an Addiction

Father, thank You for being the God who has all authority in heaven and on earth to set me free from any addiction or bad habit that has held me captive. Thank You that when Jesus conquered death on the cross, He broke the power of the enemy and that every stronghold in my mind and every force that is trying to hold me back is being broken off my life. No chain of bondage is too much or too strong for You. I believe that because the same Spirit that raised Christ from the dead lives inside me, I am Your child and a slave to nothing. I am strong, I am an overcomer, and I can do all things through Christ. I bind whatever is hindering me in the name of Jesus, and I believe my release has already happened in the unseen realm and is on the way. I'm stepping forward into full freedom and wholeness. I declare that I am free indeed. In Jesus' name, Amen.

> *"So if the Son makes you free, then you are unquestionably free."*
>
> John 8:36 AMP

To Find Direction

Father, thank You for the promise that You will guide me along the best pathways for my life if I put You first in everything I do. Thank You that You've given me Your Word as a lamp to my feet and a light to my path, and You've given me an inner ear to hear Your still small voice and know the right directions I should take. Help me to be sensitive to hear with clarity, to hear any alarms, promptings, and suggestions, and to be quick to obey. When I feel confused and uncertain, make the path easy for me to see and the seeming detours to work to my advantage. You said if I need wisdom, I could ask and You'd freely give it, so I am asking now. Help me to make decisions that honor You. I believe that where You lead and guide is better than I've imagined. In Jesus' name, Amen.

> *I will instruct you and teach you in the way you should go; I will counsel you with my loving eye on you.*
>
> Psalm 32:8 NIV

To Forgive Someone

Father, thank You that You are merciful and forgiving, that You have forgiven me and cleansed away the poison of my own sins and set me free. Thank You for showing me Your grace, Your kindness, and Your goodness over and over when I haven't deserved it, and that I can do the same with others. Help me to always forgive others quickly for anything they've done wrong to me, releasing them from past offenses and hurts before bitterness can come in. I will not wait for the other person to ask for forgiveness or do what I think they should, but I will leave any offenses in Your hands and move forward. Help me to have a heart that is free from harboring resentment and bitterness and free from being vindictive. I declare that I want to love others with Your love and cover their faults and weaknesses. In Jesus' name, Amen.

> *Make allowance for each other's faults, and forgive anyone who offends you. Remember, the Lord forgave you, so you must forgive others.*
>
> Colossians 3:13 NLT

To Step Out in Faith

Father, thank You that You are the Good Shepherd who calls me to listen for Your voice and follow You. Thank You that You are worthy of my wholehearted trust and that I do not need to lean on my own understanding when You call me out of my comfort zone and lead me where I've never gone. I know that You are taking me on a journey of faith, orchestrating opportunities for me to step into my purpose, pushing and stretching me to step into the unknown and discover what is beyond my dreams. Help me to have an uncommon faith that dares to believe and take some new steps of faith and leave the familiar behind. I believe that You have something bigger, something better, something more rewarding up in front of me. In Jesus' name, Amen.

> *By an act of faith, Abraham said yes to God's call to travel to an unknown place that would become his home. When he left he had no idea where he was going.*
>
> Hebrews 11:8 MSG

To Stop Living for Others' Approval

Father, thank You that You are with me, and You say You take great delight in me and rejoice over me with singing. Thank You that I can feel good about who I am because You made me, accept me, love me, and approve me just as I am. Help me to not look to other people to tell me who I am, to be searching for love and approval by trying to please them and measure up to what they think, to let them squeeze me into their mold of being good enough. You have already told me that I am Your masterpiece and prized possession. I declare that my identity and value is securely in Your hands and I don't have to prove myself to anyone. I believe that I have Your approval and love, and that's all I need. I declare that I am fixing my heart on pleasing You first and foremost. In Jesus' name, Amen.

> *So then, take your stand! Fasten truth around your waist like a belt. Put on God's approval as your breastplate.*
> Ephesians 6:14 GW

To Take Control of Your Thoughts

Father, thank You that You have given me the power to take control of the doorway to my mind and stop allowing negative thoughts and images to enter and play over and over. Your Word says that my thoughts run my life and that You have given me the power to rule my thoughts, my attitudes, and my emotions. Help me to clear out all the clutter of negative, critical thoughts and lies and distortions about myself, my circumstances, and about You that have made their way into my mind. I will silence the thoughts that limit me and tell me what I can't do by learning the truth of Your Word so well that I know the second a lie pops up. Help me fill my mind with Your promises and dwell on what You say. I declare that I have set my mind for victory today. May Your peace always guard my heart and mind. In Jesus' name, Amen.

Fix your thoughts on what is true, and honorable, and right, and pure, and lovely, and admirable. Think about things that are excellent and worthy of praise.

Philippians 4:8 NLT

When a Child Is Off Course

Father, thank You that You are the Almighty God who loves me at all times, who pours out Your grace upon me and never gives up on me when I've failed. Thank You for Your promise of restoring a child who goes off course, that You leave the ninety-nine and go to the mountains to seek the one who is straying. I ask You for the deep love and heart of compassion that covers their offenses and weaknesses, that restores, heals, and is full of mercy to lift them. Help me to stand in the gap and cover them with prayer and speak words of faith and encouragement over them. I believe the seed of faith that was planted in their heart never dies and will blossom at some point. I declare that they are coming back, that together we will serve You, and that You will make them mighty in the land. In Jesus' name, Amen.

Train up a child in the way he should go, and when he is old he will not depart from it.

Proverbs 22:6 NKJV

When You Are Hurting

Father, thank You that You are the God of all comfort in times when I have been hurt, in times of loss, sadness, and weeping. Thank You that You feel what I feel, that You are moved with compassion, that You heal the brokenhearted and bind up my wounds. Your Word says You are always with me and that You will turn my mourning into dancing and my sorrow into joy. I believe that no matter what disappointments and pains I go through, there is a purpose for whatever comes my way and that You only allow what I can handle and what is for my good. I believe that You will find me when I am overwhelmed, wrap Your arms around me, and lavish Your grace upon me. I declare that what was meant to harm me, You will turn to my advantage. I know that joy is on the way. In Jesus' name, Amen.

Weeping may endure for a night, but joy comes in the morning.

Psalm 30:5 NKJV

When You Don't Understand

Father, thank You that You are the living God, the eternal King, whose ways and thoughts are way beyond anything I can imagine. Thank You that You are my architect and builder and that You are working through a specific plan for my life. When I'm going through things I don't understand and nothing makes sense, help me to remember that what lies ahead and is unknown to me is well known to You. In the silent seasons, in times of testing when I can't see what You're doing or where You're taking me, I will leave it in Your hands and rest assured that You are going before me, working behind the scenes, and strategically orchestrating my steps. I declare that Your way is perfect, that You are for me, and that You will make all things work together for my good. I look forward with confidence to You leading me into a bright tomorrow. In Jesus' name, Amen.

Trust GOD from the bottom of your heart; don't try to figure out everything on your own.

Proverbs 3:5 MSG

When You Face Adversity and Challenges

Father, thank You that You are my rock, my stronghold, my hiding place in times of trouble. Thank You for the promise that You have given me the power to keep calm in times of adversity, to rule over my thoughts, attitudes, and responses to challenges. When the difficulties seem too big, help me to be bold, to dare to believe that You have already equipped me with the strength to overcome opposition and outlast adversity. Help me to grow through it, to increase my faith, to let my character come up higher. I believe that the obstacles are preparing me to do something greater in my life, that the trouble is transporting me to the next level of my destiny. I declare that my eyes are fixed on You, that I am strong and can do all things through Christ. In Jesus' name, Amen.

> *God is our refuge and strength, a very present help in trouble. Therefore we will not fear though the earth gives way, though the mountains be moved into the heart of the sea.*
>
> Psalm 46:1–2 ESV

When You Feel Like a Failure

Father, thank You that You are not a faultfinding God, but You are rich in mercy because of the great love You have for us. Thank You that Your mercies are new every morning and You are making all things new, including me. You say that I am forgiven and redeemed, that every mistake and failure and mess I've made has been paid for by Jesus on the cross. I will not drag yesterday's failures into today and allow them to keep me from moving forward. I believe that Your mercy is greater than my failures. I declare that I'm making a clear break with what I did, shaking off the guilt and condemning thoughts as well as the self-pity and discouragement, and believing You for a new beginning, for a fresh start. I will not be defined by my failures but by what You say about me. I'm rising up and moving forward in victory. In Jesus' name, Amen.

Though the righteous fall seven times, they rise again.
Proverbs 24:16 NIV

When You Need a Breakthrough

Father, thank You that David called You the God of the break-through, the God who bursts through barriers like a raging flood. Thank You that You have ordained destiny moments in my life to break through the doors of bronze, the negative things that keep me stuck. You say that in times of trouble when I don't see the way out, and it's dark, that You come bursting in with light and direction. I declare that You are breaking down strongholds in my mind, that chains of depression, of anxiety, of fear, of lack, addictions, sicknesses, and struggles at work or home are being broken. I believe that You will make quick work of what should take years, changing what has seemed unchangeable. I believe breakthroughs are coming, favor is coming, healing is coming. In Jesus' name, Amen.

> *"I will break down gates of bronze and cut through bars of iron...so that you may know that I am the LORD, the God of Israel, who summons you by name."*
>
> Isaiah 45:2–3 NIV

When You Need Hope

Father, thank You that You are the God of hope and You promise to fill me with all joy and peace so that I may overflow with hope. Thank You that in the midst of a very insecure world where hopes are often dashed and it can feel like there is no reason for hope, I can hope on in faith knowing that Your plans for my life have been set, plans that are full of hope and an abundant future. You say that my expectancy in You will never be disappointed, that everything You promise is going to come to pass. I declare that my faith is firmly anchored to my hope in You and not based on what I see or feel. I believe that You are working behind the scenes, even now, to make things happen that I can't make happen. In Jesus' name, Amen.

> *When everything was hopeless, Abraham believed anyway,*
> *deciding to live not on the basis of what he saw he couldn't*
> *do but on what God said he could do.*
>
> Romans 4:18 MSG

When You Need Peace

Father, thank You that You are the Lord of peace, the Prince of peace, who promises to keep me in perfect peace when my mind is stayed on You, because I trust You. Thank You that You are the Most High God who sees every conflict, uncertainty, worry, fear, and unexpected circumstance that I will ever face. You say to let the peace of Jesus rule in my heart, so I'm letting go of the things that are stressing me out. I declare that my peace and strength are in You, knowing You are on the throne and always watching over and caring for me even in the midst of difficulties. I will live from a place of rest and not allow anyone or anything to steal my peace. All is well today. In Jesus' name, Amen.

> *"I've told you all this so that trusting me, you will be unshakable and assured, deeply at peace. In this godless world you will continue to experience difficulties. But take heart! I've conquered the world."*
>
> John 16:33 MSG

When You Need Strength to Endure

Father, thank You that You are my strength, that I am strong in You and in the strength of Your might. Thank You that Your eyes search the whole earth in order to strengthen those whose hearts are committed to You. You say that You have given me power to tread on all the power of the enemy because Your Spirit lives in me. You have promised to be with me, to strengthen me and help me, to uphold me with Your right hand. I am shaking off my weariness and taking hold of Your strength to endure, to overcome, to outlast whatever is coming against me. I believe that Your grace is sufficient to carry me through all the difficulties and temptations. Help me to keep standing strong straight through to victory and get me to where I can't go on my own. In Jesus' name, Amen.

> *But those who wait on the LORD shall renew their strength;*
> *they shall mount up with wings like eagles, they shall run*
> *and not be weary, they shall walk and not faint.*
>
> Isaiah 40:31 NKJV

When You're Weighed Down with Cares

Father, thank You that all that is in the heavens and on the earth is Yours, and You rule over all. Thank You that just as You so wonderfully care for wildflowers, Jesus says You will provide me with exactly what I need for every season I am in. Your Word tells me to lay aside all the heavy burdens of worry, hurts, regrets, feelings of unworthiness, guilt, and frustrations that creep in and keep me from being my best. I believe that You have unlimited resources, and everything I need will be released in my life at the right time because You are my source. I declare that I am calling on Your great name and turning my load of cares over to You, knowing that You can and will carry it on my behalf. I choose to rest in faith, knowing that You are in control and have this covered. In Jesus' name, Amen.

> *Then Jesus said, "Come to me, all of you who are weary and carry heavy burdens, and I will give you rest."*
> Matthew 11:28 NLT

AN INVITATION FOR FURTHER REFLECTION

Chapter One Reflections: Dare to Pray Boldly

1. Would you say that you are asking for your dreams, for the secret petitions that God has put in your heart, or mostly for small things? Take some time to reflect on your past and present experience.

2. Psalm 2:8 says, "You're my son, and today is your birthday. What do you want? Name it: Nations as a present? Continents as a prize?" (MSG). How does that compare to what you are asking for? Write out what you consider some of your ordinary prayers. How can you change them to bold prayers?

3. Read the remarkable discussion that Jesus had with the Samaritan woman in John 4:1–26. What valuable lesson can you take from the promise of asking for "living water"? What "living water" do you need right now? Write a prayer that expresses the desire of your heart.

4. Imagine that there's a huge warehouse in Heaven that has a box of blessings with your name on it. In what ways have you found your mind trying to talk you out of asking and believing for what God has for you? What can you do to change that?

5. The apostle Paul says, "God can do anything, you know—far more than you could ever imagine or guess or request in your

wildest dreams!" (Eph. 3:20 MSG). What is God showing you about Himself and His far-and-beyond favor for you? What does that tell you about the times in your life when situations look impossible?

6. Based upon what you have learned in this chapter, how can you start praying bold prayers every day? What is God speaking to you about raising your expectations, praying and believing bigger? How is He wanting to show out in your life in new ways?

Chapter Two Reflections: Blessed Indeed

1. James 4:2 says, "You do not have because you do not ask God" (NIV). Is that true in your life? What might you be missing out on today simply because you haven't asked? Why not ask?

2. Psalm 81:10 states an amazing principle: "Open wide your mouth and I will fill it" (NIV). What does that mean? How wide open would you say your mouth is? What can you do to open it wider?

3. Jesus says, "Do not fear, little flock, for it is your Father's good pleasure to give you the kingdom" (Luke 12:32 NKJV). How can believing that make a difference in the boldness of your prayers?

4. Read 1 Chronicles 4:1–10. What caused the writer to pause the genealogy and give a description of Jabez? Would the writer pause for the same reason if he were writing a genealogy for your family? What was Jabez asking when he said "indeed"? What does that tell you about the difference a bold prayer can make?

5. Read 2 Kings 2. What bold request did Elisha make, and how was that similar to Jabez's "God, bless me indeed" prayer?

How did that prayer take Elisha to his destiny? Could the same principle hold true for you?

Chapter Three Reflections: Supernatural Provision

1. "You have to prosper in your mind before you prosper in your circumstances." What does this statement mean? Would you say you have a lack mentality or an abundant mentality?
2. What was your immediate thought when you read that "The economy may go up or down, but that's not your source; God is your source"? In the daily challenges to pay the bills and provide what's needed, do you really believe that in your heart? Explain your thoughts.
3. Psalm 35:27 states, "Let them say continually, 'Let the LORD be magnified, who delights and takes pleasure in the prosperity of His servant'" (AMP). How are your words impacting your provision? In what ways do you need to get in agreement with God and make this true for you?
4. Proverbs 3:9–10 says, "Honor the LORD with your wealth, with the firstfruits of all your crops; then your barns will be filled to overflowing" (NIV). If you are going to see supernatural provision, in what ways do you have to put God first place? Are there changes you need to make in your giving?
5. Read Exodus 17:1–7. Why does God allow situations like this to occur in our lives? Have you seen God step in suddenly and meet your need when you were complaining or grumbling rather than praying and asking? What was God showing you about Himself?
6. Read Numbers 11. When Moses told God that the situation was impossible, God responded, "Has the Lord's arm been shortened?" Describe one example from your experience

when you responded to a promise from God as Moses did. What was the outcome?

7. What are you facing today that you need God's supernatural provision to supply? Don't keep carrying around a weight of worry about it. Write a prayer to the Lord and ask Him for it, then release it into His hands by faith and enter into His rest.

Chapter Four Reflections: Awaken Your Great Faith

1. The Scripture talks about different levels of faith. Read Matthew 8:23–27. Had you been in the boat, and had you seen all that Jesus had done previously, do you think your faith response would have been better than the disciples'? Explain why.

2. What was your immediate reaction to the statement, "the good news is, great faith is in you"? Do you believe that is true? To awaken your great faith, what do you have to do?

3. Read Luke 7:1–10. What was it about the Roman centurion's faith that caused Jesus to marvel and call it "great"? What did he understand about Jesus that fueled his great faith? What valuable lesson can you take from his example?

4. Read Matthew 15:21–28. How was the Canaanite woman's great faith different than the Roman centurion's? How was it similar?

5. Jesus marveled at the centurion's faith. Read Mark 6:1–6. What caused Jesus to marvel here? When God looks at you, what do you think He marvels at?

6. Read Mark 5:21–35. There were others in the crowd that needed healing that day, but this woman was the only one who was healed. What was the one thing that made her

different? If this woman could receive her miracle based solely on her faith, is there any reason why you can't receive the miracles that you need? Explain your thoughts.

7. God wants to use you in amazing ways, to bring dreams to pass that leave you in awe, to take you places that you never thought possible. What have you learned in this chapter that you will use to awaken your great faith?

Chapter Five Reflections: Seeing Beyond the Logical

1. Jesus said to Peter, "You are a dangerous trap to me. You are seeing things merely from a human point of view, not from God's" (Matt. 16:23 NLT). Why did Jesus use such a strong word? How is it a warning for every one of us?

2. Describe one example of a time when you allowed your logic to limit a dream God put on your heart. What got into your mindset to keep you from stepping forward in faith?

3. Jesus says, "Humanly speaking, it is impossible. But with God everything is possible" (Matt. 19:26 NLT). Write down a list of some of the ways God has done the impossible throughout the Scripture. Has He changed in any way since He did those things (Heb. 13:8)? Is there some reason to think He can't do the same today?

4. Read Luke 1:26–38. What lesson can you take from Mary for the times when God puts a promise on your heart that doesn't make sense? What is God saying to you that He said to her?

5. Jesus said to the Pharisees, "You spend your time judging by the wrong criteria, by human standards" (John 8:15 VOICE). They limited their perspective of Him by what they could understand. What are some of the ways we do the same every

day? Are you feeling stuck because you're seeing things only from your perspective?

6. Read Acts 28:1–6. The islanders recognized the poisonous snake and knew Paul should die. Because this is a biblical story, do you find yourself not taking the miracle seriously? What would your reaction be if the snake was hanging on your hand?

7. Read Genesis 18:1–15; 21:1–7. What was the source of Sarah's two different laughs? Describe a time when God amazed you and caused you to laugh even though you had a limited belief in what He could do.

Chapter Six Reflections: Receive When You Believe

1. Jesus says, "Whatever you ask for in prayer, believe that you have received it, and it will be yours" (Mark 11:24 NIV). When you pray for your needs, would you say that you are receiving when you're believing? Take some time to consider this. Are you asking and hoping, or asking and receiving?

2. "Now we who have believed enter that rest" (Heb. 4:3 NIV). Describe a time when you prayed and you know you received and entered into rest.

3. Read Mark 11:12–26. How does this incident with the fig tree demonstrate the principle Jesus spoke in verse 24? How does Paul's statement in 2 Corinthians 5:7 align with this?

4. You may be looking at a fig tree today that still has all its leaves on it even though you've believed and received. What does God see, and what do you need to remind yourself about what has already happened?

5. Do you find yourself asking God for the same thing over and over again? What is that showing? What change in your thinking will help you improve in this area?

6. Read 1 John 5:14–15. What source do you have that provides God's will for your life with complete clarity? What value do you put on that in your daily schedule? Do you make time to build your confidence and faith through a deeper understanding of His Word?

7. How is James 1:5–7 in perfect agreement with Mark 11:24? Is there any reason to believe that God is reluctant to give you wisdom or anything else that is His will? What encouragement does this give you to help you receive when you believe?

Chapter Seven Reflections: Unquestionably Free

1. The Scripture says, "So if the Son makes you free, then you are unquestionably free" (John 8:36 AMP). What does it mean to be unquestionably, absolutely free indeed? Would you say that it is true in your life? In what ways are you free, and in what ways are you not?

2. Read Exodus 3:7–8. What does that tell you about whatever is hindering you, binding you, keeping you stuck? What is God about to do, and where is He taking you to? What assurance and hope does this promise give you for today and for the future?

3. God says, "Now, behold, I release you today from the chains on your hands" (Jer. 40:4 ESV). Name some of these chains. In the past, what has happened to your efforts to remove chains that need to come off you?

4. According to Romans 8:1–16 and Isaiah 9:4, what is the only way to become unquestionably free? Where does this need to start for you? How do you get in agreement with God about this?

5. Read John 5:1–17. Most of us are dealing with a lingering disorder, with a problem that won't go away. What does this

man's healing tell you about any lingering disorder you may be struggling with? What are some of the reasons you've used in the past for not getting well, not overcoming it?

6. What does the law in Deuteronomy 15:12–18 state? What does this show you about being unquestionably free? How do you feel knowing that you are coming into your seventh year?

7. What has God been saying to you about living in freedom throughout this chapter? Write a summary of His thoughts toward you.

Chapter Eight Reflections: Believing Without a Sign

1. Describe what Hebrews 11:1 means in practical terms when you're praying and believing but nothing is changing. What do you have to do in the times when God seems silent?

2. Read John 20:24–29. Do you think you would have reacted to Jesus' resurrection different than Thomas? In what way? What can you learn from his experience?

3. In 2 Kings 20:1–11, how did Hezekiah react to the bad news that Isaiah delivered? What remarkable message does this tell you about the life-changing power of prayer? How do you feel knowing this?

4. What is the problem with always being dependent on a sign? How much do you struggle with wanting signs? What is the right perspective to have?

5. Read 1 Kings 18:41–46. What does that tell you about the things God will put in your spirit? What do you have to do when you're standing in faith for rain but all you see is blue sky? Have you experienced a moment like that when a small cloud finally rises up and it's soon followed by a remarkable rainstorm? What was that like?

6. Read Acts 12:1–10. What does verse 7 tell you about times when all the odds are against you? Why does God arrange for the times when we have to wait, believe, and not be moved by what we don't see?

7. What lesson can you take from Simeon's experience in Luke 2:22–32 that will help you to pray bolder now and in the future?

Chapter Nine Reflections: Pray for Others

1. The Scripture says, "Pray for one another... The prayer of a righteous person has great power as it is working" (James 5:16 ESV). What are some obvious needs that you see in the people God has put in your life? How do you feel knowing that your prayers for them have great power to bring change in their lives?

2. Read Job 42:7–17. Even when you have great needs yourself, what valuable lesson on praying boldly for others can you take from Job's example?

3. The apostle Paul says, "Bear one another's burdens, and so fulfill the law of Christ" (Gal. 6:2 NKJV). What does that mean? How does prayer play a role in that? In what ways have you made this a part of your daily life?

4. What was your immediate response to the statement "Prayer moves the hands that rule the world"? Do you actually believe that about your prayers? If you do, have you been taking it seriously? Given this power of prayer, in what ways are you using it?

5. Read Ezekiel 22:30. What did it mean to stand in the gap back then? What does it mean for you today? Name one person for whom you will stand in the gap and cover them in prayer until their broken-down walls are repaired.

6. Read Exodus 32:1–14, then Psalm 106:23. What is Moses credited with doing? How serious can it be to stand in the gap for others? What amazing thing happened when he stood in the gap for the Israelites? Do you think that in certain situations your prayers can do the same?

7. It's easy to look at someone who's doing wrong and give up hope for them. We may not even be aware that we've written them off as a lost cause. Does someone in your life come to your mind? What message does Moses have for you?

Chapter Ten Reflections: Keep Believing for Your Loved Ones

1. Read Acts 8:1–3; 9:1–19. Had you been aware of Saul before he became Paul, would you have ever dreamed that he could change? Do you think you would have responded as Ananias did and reach out to an enemy such as Saul?

2. Give a description of the Samaritan woman in John 4:1–26. How did Jesus treat her? Do you tend to find yourself trying to avoid people who are living "messed up"?

3. Do you have a child or loved one who's off course and needs you to wait on them, to keep believing for them? Read 1 Corinthians 13:4–8. "Love never fails." As you wait on someone in need, in what ways can you love them back on track?

4. Read the story of the prodigal son in Luke 15:11–31. In waiting on his son, how did this father show his love? If you were the father, do you see yourself responding as he did? What is our role to be toward the prodigal, and what is the Holy Spirit's role?

5. According to John 13:35, what is the most important thing to do for others? Describe a time when someone came alongside you and just loved and supported you when you needed to

change rather than confront you and tell you how wrong you were. What was the outcome?

6. Read Luke 19:1–11. What was Zacchaeus's reputation? Yet what was he seeking that day? What does that tell you about what's going on inside another person's life? Would you have invited yourself to his house as Jesus did? What lesson can you take from Jesus' example?

Chapter Eleven Reflections: Remember What God Said

1. What does 2 Corinthians 1:20 state is always true? Describe one of God's promises to you that has not come to pass and the enemy keeps tempting you to live frustrated, worried, or afraid. How do you counter that? How do you stay in faith?

2. Read John 11:17–44. At the seemingly most hopeless moment, what did Jesus say to Martha? When you're discouraged or stressed out and worried about something, what has God said that will defeat those negative thoughts?

3. In Job 8:20–21; 19:23–27, what did Job do and say to make it through the difficult time of the great loss of his children, his business, and his health? At the end of Job's test in Job 42:12–17, how did he come out? What does that tell you about the times when you are being tested?

4. Read Luke 24:1–10. What turned these women's discouragement, sorrow, and defeat into hope and passion? Describe a difficult time when you experienced something similar.

5. Describe the scene on the water from Peter's vantage point in Matthew 14:22–33. What could possibly have inspired him to get out of the boat? Is there a situation in your life that Jesus is calling you to walk on water? What would that look like?

6. Read Nehemiah 1–2. When Nehemiah took a bold step of faith, what did God do for him, and what did he accomplish? What will God do for you when you do the same?

7. Peter walked on water. Nehemiah rebuilt the walls of Jerusalem. What is it that you believe God wants to do through your life?

Chapter Twelve Reflections: God Has the Final Say

1. According to Romans 8:31–32, what does God being for you mean in practical terms?

2. Read Daniel 3. What is true of children of the Most High God even when they face what look like impossible situations? What does this say to you about the times you feel the need to play up to people to be accepted and valued?

3. If people have the final say, what would have happened to David in 1 Samuel 16:1–13? What does this tell you about what God has purposed for your life?

4. Take some time to meditate on this amazing statement: "Jesus has the last word on everything and everyone, from angels to armies. He's standing right alongside God, and what He says goes" (1 Pet. 3:22 MSG). What are your thoughts on its implication for your life?

5. Read Romans 4:19–21. When God puts something in your heart that you think could never happen, what can you learn from Abraham's experience that will help you? How do you stay in agreement with God?

6. In Genesis 39–41, what say did Joseph's brothers, Potiphar, and the prisoner whose dream Joseph interpreted have in his life? What happened when God had the final say? What does that tell you about whatever is hindering you?

7. Read John 11:1–44. Has it ever seemed like you prayed and stood in faith, but God showed up too late for you? Why the period of silence when you seem to need Him the most? What needs to happen as you wait?

8. When Jesus took His last breath on the cross and died, the enemy celebrated what appeared to be their victory over the Son of God. What did they fail to take into account? What lesson can you take from that to help you to keep praying bold prayers that move the hands that rule the world?

ACKNOWLEDGMENTS

In this book I offer many stories shared with me by friends, members of our congregation, and people I've met around the world. I appreciate and acknowledge their contributions and support. Some of those mentioned in the book are people I have not met personally, and in a few cases, we've changed the names to protect the privacy of individuals. I give honor to all those to whom honor is due. As the son of a church leader and a pastor myself, I've listened to countless sermons and presentations, so in some cases I can't remember the exact source of a story.

I am indebted to the amazing staff of Lakewood Church, the wonderful members of Lakewood who share their stories with me, and those around the world who generously support our ministry and make it possible to bring hope to a world in need. I am grateful to all those who follow our services on television, the Internet, SiriusXM, and through the podcasts. You are all part of our Lakewood family.

I offer special thanks also to all the pastors across the country who are members of our Champions Network.

Once again, I am grateful for a wonderful team of professionals who helped me put this book together for you. Leading them is my FaithWords/Hachette publisher, Daisy Hutton, along with Patsy Jones and the team at FaithWords. I truly appreciate the editorial contributions of wordsmith Lance Wubbels, and a special thanks to Phil Munsey for his insights and friendship.

204 *Acknowledgments*

I am grateful also to my literary agents Jan Miller Rich and Shannon Marven at Dupree Miller & Associates.

And last but not least, thanks to my wife, Victoria, and our children, Alexandra and Jonathan and his wife, Sophia, who are my sources of daily inspiration. Thanks as well to our closest family members, who serve as day-to-day leaders of our ministry, including my mother, Dodie; my brother, Paul, and his wife, Jennifer; my sister Lisa and her husband, Kevin; and my brother-in-law Don and his wife, Jackelyn.

WE WANT TO HEAR FROM YOU!

Each week, I close our international television broadcast by giving the audience an opportunity to make Jesus the Lord of their lives. I'd like to extend that same opportunity to you. Are you at peace with God? A void exists in every person's heart that only God can fill. I'm not talking about joining a church or finding religion. I'm talking about finding life and peace and happiness. Would you pray with me today? Just say, "Lord Jesus, I repent of my sins. I ask You to come into my heart. I make You my Lord and Savior."

Friend, if you prayed that simple prayer, I believe you have been "born again." I encourage you to attend a good Bible-based church and keep God in first place in your life. For free information on how you can grow stronger in your spiritual life, please feel free to contact us.

Victoria and I love you, and we'll be praying for you. We're believing for God's best for you, that you will see your dreams come to pass. We'd love to hear from you!

To contact us, write to:

Joel and Victoria Osteen
PO Box #4271
Houston, TX 77210

Or you can reach us online at joelosteen.com.